Travel Guide

GRAN CANARIA

ROWLAND MEAD

NEW
HOLLAND

D0263398

NEW
HOLLAND

★★★ Highly recommended
★★ Recommended
★ See if you can

First edition published in 2002
by New Holland Publishers (UK) Ltd
London • Cape Town • Sydney • Auckland

10 9 8 7 6 5 4 3 2 1

website: www.newhollandpublishers.com

Garfield House, 86 Edgware Road
London W2 2EA
United Kingdom

80 McKenzie Street
Cape Town 8001
South Africa

14 Aquatic Drive
Frenchs Forest, NSW 2086
Australia

218 Lake Road
Northcote, Auckland
New Zealand

Distributed in the USA by
The Globe Pequot Press
Connecticut

ISBN 1 84330 096 6

Publishing Manager: John Loubser
Managing Editor: Thea Grobbelaar
DTP Cartographic Manager: Genené Hart
Publishing Manager (UK): Simon Pooley
Editor: Jacqueline de Villiers
Design and DTP: Lellyn Creamer
Cartographer: Marisa Galloway
Proofreader: Glynne Newlands
Consultant: Sue Bryant
Picture Researcher: Colleen Abrahams

Reproduction by Hirt & Carter (Pty) Ltd, Cape Town
Printed and bound in Hong Kong by Sing Cheong
Printing Co. Ltd.

Photographic Credits:
ffotograff: cover, pages 9, 11, 14, 16, 19, 20, 23, 26, 27,
34 (top and bottom), 39, 40, 43, 59, 87, 89, 91, 92, 93, 104;
Jenny Forest: title page, pages 7, 10, 67, 102, 112;
Rowland Mead: pages 6, 8, 48, 74, 90, 105, 108, 111,
114, 115 (top), 116, 117;
PhotoBank/Adrian Baker: pages 4, 36, 50, 54, 64, 65,
66, 84;
PhotoBank/Peter Baker: pages 24, 82;
Brian Richards: pages 29, 98, 101, 103, 106;
Jeroen Snijders: pages 12, 15, 17, 18, 28, 30, 31, 32, 33,
35, 42, 44, 45, 46, 47, 51, 56, 58, 60, 61, 62, 63, 70, 73,
75, 76, 77, 78, 79 (top and bottom), 80, 115 (bottom),
118, 119;
Travel Ink/Mike Nicholson: page 25;
Travel Ink/Mike Pollitt: pages 21, 113;
Travel Ink/Andrew Watson: pages 94, 95.

Although every effort has been made to ensure
accuracy of facts, and telephone and fax numbers
in this book, the publishers will not be held
responsible for changes that occur at the time of
going to press.

Cover: *An active yacht harbour and fishing port,
Puerto de Mogán.*
Title Page: *The attractive resort of Taurito, on the
southwest coast of Gran Canaria.*

CONTENTS

1. Introducing Gran Canaria 5
The Land 6
History in Brief 13
Government and Economy 21
The People 23

**2. Las Palmas de
Gran Canaria 37**
History 38
Vegueta 40
Triana 44
The Central Area of Las Palmas 47
Northern Las Palmas 48

3. The North 55
The Coast 56
Guanche Connections 58
Inland 61

4. The Arid East 71
Commuter Country 72
Telde 75
Ingenio 77
Agüimes 78
The Arid Coastal Strip 80

5. The South 83
The Eastern Section 84
Playa del Inglés 85
Maspalomas 86
Theme Parks and
Other Attractions 88
The West of the Region 92

6. The West 99
The Mogán Valley 100
San Nicolás de Tolentino 102
Agaete and the
Puerto de las Nieves 104

7. The Central Highlands 109
Routes into the
Central Highlands 110
Features of the
Central Highlands 114

Travel Tips 122

Index 127

1
Introducing Gran Canaria

Gran Canaria is one of seven major islands in the Canarian archipelago. Covering 1532km² (591 square miles), it is the third largest of the islands and has the largest population. Gran Canaria is almost circular in shape and measures some 45km (28 miles) across. The inhabitants like to refer to it as a **continent in miniature**. It has a wide variety of scenery; the central mountains, which rise to 1945m (6382ft) at the **Pico de las Nieves**, are volcanic in origin and the fertile valleys, called *barrancos*, radiate out like the spokes of a wheel. In other areas there are verdant pine forests, luxuriant banana plantations and steep terraced slopes, while the low-lying southeast of the island consists of arid semidesert reminiscent of the Sahara. The coastline is also varied with towering cliffs in the west, rocky shore-lines – interspersed with sandy bays – in the east and a huge area of sand dunes at Maspalomas.

Bathed by the warm Atlantic waters, freshened by the trade winds and blessed by almost perpetual sunshine, Gran Canaria has been described as the 'land of eternal spring'. Little wonder that it has become a year-round tourist destination.

Visitors flock to the drier south of the island, where purpose-built resorts such as **Playa del Inglés** and **Maspalomas** provide entertainment, nightlife, theme parks and predictable sunshine. The steady wind and impressive waves also make this an ideal area for water sports such as windsurfing and sailing. Hikers, on the other hand, prefer the central part of the island where

ATLANTIC OCEAN

Lanzarote
Santa Cruz   Arrecife
La de la Palma   Santa Cruz
Palma   de Tenerife   Puerto del
San Sebastián   Tenerife   Rosario
de la Gomera●   Las Palmas   Fuerteventura
● La Gomera   de Gran Canaria
●Valverde
El Hierro   Gran Canaria

TOP ATTRACTIONS

*** **Cathedral of Santa Ana:** the Canary Islands' only cathedral in Las Palmas..
*** **Museo Canario:** interesting information on the Guanche way of life at this museum in Las Palmas.
** **Teror:** visit the spiritual heart of the island.
** **Las Dunas de Maspalomas:** a huge spread of sand dunes in the middle of this southern resort.
** **Barranco de Guayadeque:** Guanche caves and rare plants in this spectacular gorge.

Opposite: *The exquisite Catedral de Santa Ana in Las Palmas.*

Above: *View from the Pico de Bandama, an ancient volcano rising to 574m (1883ft).*
Opposite: *Layers of volcanic rock near Roque Nublo in the centre of the island.*

there is a network of country paths, many of which feature ancient sites.

Dominating the north of the island is the capital **Las Palmas** – a sophisticated, cosmopolitan city and busy port. Many tourists spend a day here visiting the shops, the museums and the cathedral. The north of Gran Canaria has some fine old towns, such as **Telde**, **Teror** and **Gáldar**, which have connections not only with the Spanish conquistadors, but with the original inhabitants of the island known as the **Guanches**.

Gran Canaria has a lot to offer the visitor and it is fortunate that the island has a good infrastructure and the roads allow for easy exploration. A motorway runs halfway round the island, rental cars are cheap and coach excursions are easily arranged. Whatever the interests of the visitor, Gran Canaria has something to suit all needs for an exciting holiday.

THE LAND

Gran Canaria is one of the **Canary Islands**, an archipelago lying some 300km (186 miles) west of the African coast of Morocco. The islands belong to Spain, which is situated 1120km (696 miles) northeast. Gran Canaria lies on latitude 28° north, some 480km (298 miles) from the Tropic of Cancer, and in addition to Gran Canaria, there are six other islands in the archipelago – Tenerife, Lanzarote, Fuerteventura, La Palma, La Gomera and El Hierro (as well as some uninhabited islets). Together the Canary Islands cover approximately 7500km² (2895 square miles) and they belong – geographically – to **Macronesia**, which is a group of islands (including Madeira and the Azores) of similar volcanic origins, topography and indigenous flora and fauna. The Canary Islands are around 40 million years old and were formed during the Tertiary Geological Era (the time the Atlas

---

FACT FILE

Size: 1560km² (602 square miles).
Population: 760,000.
Capital: Las Palmas is the capital of both Gran Canaria and the eastern province of the Canary Islands.
Position: 210km (130 miles) west of the African coast, 17°W and 27°N.
Time Zone: GMT (plus one hour in summer).
Language: Spanish.
Currency: Euro.
Religion: Roman Catholic.
Highest Mountain: Pico de las Nieves 1949m (6395ft).
Tourism: 2,200,000 visitors each year.

Mountains in north Africa were formed) when the African tectonic plate moved northeast and created a weakness in the earth's crust through which volcanic material poured. The Canary Islands can thus be thought of as the tips of underwater volcanoes. Fortunately, there is little volcanic activity in the Canary Islands today, and volcanoes are regarded as extinct on Gran Canaria and Fuerteventura. The last eruptions took place on Lanzarote in 1824, on Tenerife in 1909 and, the most recent eruption, on La Palma in 1971. Gran Canaria, nevertheless, is filled with manifestations of former volcanic activity, which add to the fascination of its varied scenery.

THE NAME 'CANARY'

Controversy has always raged about the origin of the name 'Canary'. It is true that there are wild canaries throughout the archipelago, but these birds probably got their name from the islands, rather than the other way round. A popular theory is that early settlers were impressed by the size of the dogs on the islands and used the Latin word for dogs (*canus*) to name the area. A further supposition is that the primitive inhabitants of the islands were Berbers from the Canarii tribe in Morocco. Take your pick!

Mountains and Rivers

The highest part of Gran Canaria is at its centre, where certain points are over 1500m (4922ft) in height and can attract a good covering of snow in the winter months. It is possible to drive right to the summit of the loftiest peak – **Pico** (or Pozo) **de las Nieves** – which reaches a height of 1949m (6395ft). There are also some spectacular

PLATE TECTONICS AND VOLCANOES

The fairly new science of **plate tectonics** has done much to explain the distribution of the world's volcanoes. Derived from the theory of the **Continental Drift**, this science proves that the earth's crust is divided into movable plates. The plate boundaries are lines of weakness through which volcanic magma pours. This explains the series of volcanoes in mid-Atlantic regions, such as Iceland and the Azores, where the American and European plates are moving apart. The Canary Islands are not on the mid-Atlantic ridge, but lie in an area of the crust's weakness. This was caused by the movement of the African plate drifting towards the east, and that built up the nearby Atlas Mountains in North Africa.

peaks, which are the cores or spines of ancient volcanoes. These include **Roque Nublo** – peaking at 1817m (5962ft) – and **Roque Bentaiga** – at 1412m (4633ft). The Central Highlands extend westwards to the coast and form a spectacular, but often inaccessible, shoreline. Radiating out from the Central Highlands is a series of deep valleys called *barrancos* (*see* page 112). Today these valleys are mainly dry (there are no permanent rivers on Gran Canaria) and they were probably formed in wetter climatic times such as the period immediately after the ice age. The water table is often close to the floor of the *barrancos* and many of these valleys are filled with subtropical crops such as bananas, papayas and sugar cane. In many places the *barrancos* have been dammed to form *embalses* (reservoirs) to provide much needed water to Las Palmas and the tourist resorts in the south.

A different type of landscape can be found on the southeastern side of Gran Canaria, which lies in the rain shadow of the mountains. Here, the low rainfall and lack of trees has created an area of arid **semidesert**, which has much in common with the Sahara nearly 300km (186 miles) to the east in Africa.

Seas and Shores

The deep waters of the Atlantic Ocean surround Gran Canaria and its erosive power shapes the coastline. Over time the waves have worked on the volcanic rocks, producing the island's varied shoreline. The eastern coast is generally low-lying, but the west coast has some spectacular cliffs, particularly between Agaete and the Punta de la Aldea. Gran Canaria's beaches vary tremendously. They are often strewn with boulders or consist of coarse black volcanic sand. The best yellow-sand beaches can be found at

Below: *Playa de las Canteras lies on the western side of Las Palmas, the capital of Gran Canaria.*

Playa de las Canteras at Las Palmas and along the south coast from Playa del Cardón to Puerto Rico. In many cases, however, the sand has been imported from the Sahara Desert, as the island's existing sand was coarse, black volcanic material or there was no sand at all.

Above: *A typical tourist development in the south of the island.*

Fortunately, the shortage of decent beaches is not a handicap, as most apartments and hotels have excellent pools and in other areas seawater lido complexes (man-made swimming pools and landscaped water features along a sea front) have been built. One unusual coastal feature is the **dune complex at Maspalomas**. These sand ridges cover some 4km² (1.5 square miles) and when a caravan of tourists passes by on camels it seems as if you are in the Sahara Desert. The small lagoon or *charca* alongside the dunes is one of the few coastal wetlands in Gran Canaria. The Atlantic shoreline also ensures that almost every type of **water sport** imaginable is catered for, including surfing, sail boarding, deep-sea fishing and scuba diving.

Climate

The climate of Gran Canaria, along with that of the other Canary Islands, has been described as that of everlasting spring, although at some of the island's southern resorts it is more like continual summer. There is, in fact, considerable climatic variety on the island depending on the geographical position and the height of the land. The moist **trade winds** blow from the north, so that the windward northern coast has more rain and cloud than the rest of the island. The leeward south and southeast of Gran Canaria are drier and hotter. These areas may have as many as 2500 hours of **sunshine** a year and it is here where many tourist developments have recently been established. **Temperatures** vary from 18–24°C (65–75°F)

TRADE WINDS AND CLOUDS

One of the features of Gran Canaria that fascinates visitors arriving by plane is the persistent layer of cloud lying above 500m (1641ft). The clouds are formed by the moist **trade winds**, which blow off the Atlantic Ocean from a northeasterly direction for much of the year. As these winds reach the land they are forced to rise against the mountains and then cool and condense forming clouds. It is these winds that bring the rain and moisture that provides the rich growing conditions for the luxuriant vegetation in the north of Gran Canaria. Tourists should not worry too much about the clouds, which rarely cover the sunny resorts in the south of the island, but they should choose a cloud-free day to head inland to the mountainous centre of Gran Canaria.

Above: *Bougainvillea and other colourful shrubs are a feature of hotel gardens.*

in the summer and 16–20°C (61–68°F) in the winter, although afternoon temperatures during both seasons can be markedly higher. Occasionally, during the summer, the hot sirocco wind blows from the Sahara and brings desert dust, high temperatures and discomfort to all. Locals refer to this phenomenon as *Tiempo Africano* (African weather).

Rainfall is generally light and varies from 750mm (29.5 inches) on the north coast to 250mm (9.9 inches) in the south. One interesting feature of the climate of Gran Canaria is the layer of **cloud**, which is brought by the trade winds and lies on the windward side of the island above 500m (1641ft). It may burn off in the afternoon, but can last for days, providing light rain, which benefits the various forms of agriculture in the region. The final climatic factor is the cool **Canary Current**. This flows from the north and ensures that the sea temperatures around the island are lower than what might be expected at this latitude. The sea temperature is around 18°C (64.5°F) in the winter and it increases to 22°C (71°F) in the summer.

Flora

The varied altitude levels, the rich volcanic soil and the amenable climate combine to make Gran Canaria a botanist's paradise. There are a huge number of plants that are indigenous to the Canary Islands and other flora includes the species of Mediterranean origin, brought by the Spaniards after the Conquest (*see* page 15), and exotic plants brought to the islands by sailors and travellers from all over the world.

In the arid semidesert areas in the south of Gran Canaria, drought-resistant plants form scrubland. Especially common are the *euphorbias* or **spurges**.

THE LEGEND OF ATLANTIS

Theories about the lost continent of Atlantis in Greek and Roman mythology suggest that a large continent, called Atlantis, lay somewhere to the west of Gibraltar. It was thought to be some sort of Utopia, but it had almost entirely slipped beneath the waves and disappeared. Plato, probably basing his evidence on the stories of mariners, claimed that only seven mountaintops remained above the waves. It is probably no coincidence that the seven main islands of the Canaries all have volcanic peaks and that new volcanic islands of soft ash can easily be washed away by the sea. Could the Canary Islands be the legendary lost continent of Atlantis?

Growing widely are the candelabra spurge (which looks very much like a cactus) and the various species of Canary spurge. In the south of Gran Canaria many plants, such as **tomatoes** and **bananas**, are grown under plastic with the aid of irrigation (*see* page 80). In the wetter north, the lower land is characterized by a wide variety of subtropical and tropical crops, which include **oranges**, **dates** and **sugar cane**. The towns and cities are bright with flowers and shrubs, such as **bougainvillea**, **hibiscus**, **geraniums** and **strelitzia** (or bird of paradise plant), and colourful trees, such as **jacaranda** and **mimosa**. Some hotel landscapes resemble botanical gardens. At higher levels, where cloud is more frequent, **Canarian pines**, **eucalyptus** and **cork oak** are common, while **poinsettas** grow like weeds along the roadsides.

Crops such as **grapes**, **potatoes** and **cereals** are grown at these levels. No account of the flora of Gran Canaria would be complete without a mention of the remarkable **dragon tree** (*Dracaena draco*). Some specimens reach 18m (59ft) in height and can live for hundreds of years. These trees were undoubtedly around during the times of the Guanches, who regarded them as sacred.

> ### THE USEFUL DRAGON TREE
>
> Of all the exotic trees in Gran Canaria, it is the **dragon tree** (*Dracæna draco*) which is the most interesting and mysterious. The trees are believed to live for several centuries, but it is impossible to date them precisely as they do not produce tree rings. The tree has survived the ice age and is a remnant of the Tertiary era flora. Traditionally, Guanche meetings took place under a dragon tree. They also used its sap (called dragon's blood, as it turns bright red when exposed to air) to heal wounds, ward off evil spirits and embalm their dead. The sap is also believed to be a cure for leprosy, and it was once exported to Italy to stain marble and violins.

Fauna

In contrast to the superb flora, the animal life of Gran Canaria is disappointing. Only 56 species of **birds** have been recorded as breeding in the Canary Islands, as a whole, and the figure for Gran Canaria is a lot lower. Some of these have become extinct and many are only spasmodic breeders. Bird watchers will be keen to see one species that is endemic to the Canary Islands – the blue chaffinch, which is most likely to be encountered in the pine forests. In addition to these are three Macronesian endemisms – the plain swift, Berthalot's pipit and the wild canary – all of which are quite common. The only frequently seen raptors are kestrels, sparrowhawks and buzzards. Other common birds are

Below: *The Canary palm is grown throughout the Canary Islands and is frequently seen in parks and hotel gardens.*

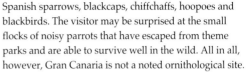

Spanish sparrows, blackcaps, chiffchaffs, hoopoes and blackbirds. The visitor may be surprised at the small flocks of noisy parrots that have escaped from theme parks and are able to survive well in the wild. All in all, however, Gran Canaria is not a noted ornithological site.

Amongst the **amphibians** and **reptiles** on the island are three gecko species, two species of frog, and one species of lizard and skink. Geckoes, regarded by the locals as signs of good luck, are often found in houses and hotel bedrooms where they prey on insects. The large Canarian lizard, of which there are a number of subspecies, is abundant on stone walls where it feeds on insects and plants.

With the exception of bats, humans have introduced all the **terrestrial mammals** in Gran Canaria. There are two species of bat, both of which are common. Rabbits, house mice, hedgehogs and black and brown rats have

been around for some time. **Marine mammals** are well represented and include a number of species of whale, porpoise and dolphin. Boat trips to watch whales and dolphins are becoming very popular at the southern resorts. There are over 400 species of **fish** in the Atlantic around the Canary Islands. They include various types of shark, tuna, stingrays and many of the fish that appear on the menus in restaurants, such as hake, sardines and swordfish. Common shellfish include lobsters, prawns and mussels.

There is a wide range of **insects**, including the unwelcome mosquito (although it is not the malaria-carrying type). Dragonflies, including the common scarlet darter, inhabit the wetter regions. Amongst the endemic butterflies are the Canarian versions of the red admiral, grayling, speckled wood and Cleopatra. Migrating monarchs can be seen in abundance at certain times of the year.

HISTORY IN BRIEF

The early history of the Canary Islands is shrouded in mythology and mystery. The Greeks and Romans certainly knew of the islands' existence as Plato thought that they were the remains of the lost continent of Atlantis, and the Greek astronomer, Ptolemy, accurately located their position in AD150. But it is highly unlikely that the Greeks or the Romans set foot on the Canary Islands, yet the Phoenicians and the Carthaginians most certainly did.

Early Inhabitants

Remains of **Cro-Magnon man** have been found in the Canary Islands and examinations of skulls, showing people with broad faces and high foreheads, have been carbon dated to 3000BC. When European exploration of the islands took place in the 14th century, they found a primitive people living there who were tall, blond and blue-eyed. Although they were probably known as the *Canarios* on Gran Canaria, the Tenerife name of **Guanches** has been adopted to describe the indigenous

Opposite: *Children on the Canary Islands often make pets of the common lizard.*

THE NEW YEAR

It is a tradition in Spain, including Gran Canaria, to place more emphasis on New Year celebrations than those of Christmas. At the stroke of midnight on New Year's Eve, it is custom to drink champagne (*cava*) and eat a grape for each stroke of the clock. To consume 12 grapes and take a drink so quickly is not easy and usually leads to much laughter. The 12 grapes are supposed to guarantee good times in the year ahead.

HISTORICAL CALENDAR

3000BC Archaeological evidence suggests that Gran Canaria was inhabited by Cro-Magnon man.
1100BC Phoenicians and Carthaginians visited the Canary Islands.
1312 Genoese explorer Lanzarotto Malocello occupies and names Lanzarote.
1340 Portugal and Spain send ships to explore the islands and find the Guanches living a Stone Age existence.
1401 Spanish Conquest begins with Jean de Béthencourt defeating Lanzarote, and then La Gomera and Fuerteventura.
1478 Juan Réjon attacks Gran Canaria, but it takes a further

five years to overpower the Guanches.
1483 Pedro de Viera is appointed the first governor of the Canary Islands.
1492 Columbus makes his first visit to the Canary Islands and observes Mount Teide erupting.
1494 Tenerife is the last island to be conquered by the Spanish.
16th and 17th centuries The Spanish colonize the islands, with settlers establishing a thriving economy, aided by the slave trade. Pirates and navies of rival countries pose a constant threat.
1852 Isabella II declares the Canaries a free trade zone. In

the late 19th century bananas replace sugar as the mainstay of the economy.
1927 Canary Islands are divided into two provinces, with Las Palmas as the capital of the eastern province, consisting of Gran Canaria, Lanzarote and Fuerteventura.
1936 General Franco plots a military coup, which leads to the Spanish Civil War.
1982 Regional Constitution granted by Spain to the Canary Islands.
1986 Canary Islands gain special status within the European Union.
2002 The abolition of the Spanish peseta.

people of all the Canary Islands. The origins of the Guanches and how they arrived on the islands is not certain, as they appear to have had no knowledge of boat building, yet most experts now believe that they were Berbers from North Africa.

Above: *Detailed stonework adorns a wooden-framed window of the Casa de Colón, once the home of Christopher Columbus, now a museum.*
Opposite: *There is a fine collection of Guanche skulls in the Museo Canario in Las Palmas.*

Guanche Society

The Europeans found a primitive, Stone Age society – with no knowledge of metals, the wheel, boat building or the bow and arrow – living on the islands. The majority of the inhabitants lived in caves, which were easily carved out of soft volcanic ash. There are some fine examples of these caves on Gran Canaria, which include the **Cueva Pintada** (or Painted Cave) at Gáldar. It appears that on Gran Canaria house dwelling was a symbol of high status and more Guanches here lived in simple stone houses than on any of the other islands. Their economy was based on animal rearing and the cultivating of crops such as grain. The women made elaborately decorated pots using the coil method rather than the wheel. Their clothing was made from sheep and goat skins and these animals also provided meat, cheese and milk to the Guanches' diet of fish, fruit and *gofio* (roasted grain flour).

Despite their primitive way of life, the Guanches had a sophisticated social structure. Gran Canaria was divided into two kingdoms that were based around the towns of Telde and Gáldar. The two kings were known as *guanatemes*, who shared power with a *faycan* or priest, and they were advised by a number of nobles who were clan chiefs. The boundary between the two kingdoms on Gran Canaria is believed to have passed through Roque Bentaiga and Roque Nublo, which were both held sacred by the Guanches. Justice was administered through a council that usually met under an ancient dragon tree. The Guanches were monogamous and women played a vital role in their society, often becoming a *faycan* or a *guanateme*. There was no death penalty, but murderers were severely beaten and their possessions were given to the relatives of their victims as compensation. The Guanches worshipped a god known as *Achaman*, who was closely associated with the sun, and mummified those belonging to the highest social strata, using skins and reeds, before laying them in special burial caves.

The Spanish Conquest

The conquest of the Canary Islands by the Europeans began in 1312, when a Genoese explorer named **Lanzarotto Malocello** conquered, and gave his name to, Lanzarote. This event was followed by years of squabbling between Portugal and Spain over the ownership of the islands, which ended in 1401 with the islands being incorporated into the Spanish crown. The European conquest continued in earnest the following year when **Jean de Béthencourt** took Lanzarote for the King of Castile. By 1406 Béthencourt had also conquered Fuerteventura and La Gomera. This was no great feat as the small Guanche population on these islands had been decimated through many years of slave trading. The more dominant islands of Gran Canaria and Tenerife were then prepared to provide a more determined resistance.

Spain began the second phase of the conquest in 1478 when Fernando and Isabella sanctioned an attack on Gran Canaria by **Juan Réjon**. (The Catholic monarchs were known as *Los Reyes Católicos* and

THE ORIGIN OF THE GUANCHES

A great anthropological mystery concerns the origin of the Guanches. One idea suggests that they came from mainland Europe, prompted by the fact that many of the Guanches had fair hair and blue eyes. The other theory is that they came from north Africa and were of Berber origin. The question of how they arrived at the islands still remains, as there is no evidence suggesting that the Guanches knew how to build boats. Thor Heyerdahl is the Norwegian explorer who built and sailed reed rafts to prove the migration of ancient civilisations. He believes that the Guanches arrived in the Canary Islands on reed boats and since there are no suitable reeds on the islands, this boat-building skill must have died out. The north African theory is supported by the fact that the Guanches mummified their dead and possibly even built pyramids.

they were responsible for driving the Moors out of mainland Spain. After this they turned their attention to overseas colonization and sponsored Columbus on his voyages.) Réjon encountered a fierce resistance from the Guanches and it took five years before they were defeated. **Pedro de Vera**, who arrived as the military governor in 1480, eventually replaced Réjon. His methods were more aggressive and if the legend holds true, he slew one of the most important Guanche chiefs with his own hands. De Vera eventually overcame the northern kingdom and converted the king, **Tenesor Semidan**, to Christianity. Semidan persuaded many of his subjects to do likewise and many Guanches subsequently became Spanish mercenaries in the battles to come. In 1483 Gran Canaria was completely overpowered and the next Spanish commander was **Alonso Fernández de Lugo** who, in 1491, received royal assent to attack La Palma and Tenerife. La Palma was quickly taken, but Tenerife proved to be the toughest island to overcome. De Lugo arrived on the island in 1493 with a force of 1000 soldiers as well as 150 Guanche mercenaries from Gran Canaria. There were a number of battles and de Lugo had to send for extra men from Spain before Tenerife was finally defeated.

Right: *Sculptures of Canary Island dogs guard the entrance to Plaza de Santa Ana in Las Palmas.*

Left: An aerial view
of the island of Gran
Canaria, with Las
Palmas in the lower
part of the photograph.

Post-Conquest Guanches

After the Conquest, Gran Canaria and the other islands
were administered for Spain by *capitanes-generales*.
Many Guanches died from diseases introduced by the
newcomers to which they had no resistance, and large
numbers of Guanches were taken to Spain as slaves
(although many were later allowed to return). Others
interbred with the invaders, assumed Spanish names
and were converted to Christianity. Assimilation with
the colonists came swiftly and the Guanches original
spoken language quickly disappeared. Modern anthropological research, however, claims that many authentic
characteristics of the Guanches are evident in the Canary
Islands today. The inhabitants of Gran Canaria are proud
of their Guanche ancestry, as they feel that this distin-
guishes them from the mainland Spaniards.

Spanish Colonial Rule

For the next three or four centuries the Canary Islands
experienced mixed fortunes under Spanish colonial rule.
The islands attracted large numbers of settlers, not only
from Spain, but also from Portugal, France and Italy.
After Columbus's discovery of the New World in 1492,
the Gran Canaria – and particularly its chief port Las
Palmas – became an important staging post for ships
travelling to and from the Americas. Any territory owned
by Spain, however, was fair game for corsairs. The

VERDINO DOGS

It is often claimed that the
Canary Islands acquired their
name from the Latin word
canus (dog). Historical records
often mention the large dogs
that were once found on the
islands and some researchers
suggest that the inhabitants
actually ate the dogs.
Certainly, the Spanish
Conquistadors found that
the Guanches did keep rather
fierce dogs that were used to
guard their flocks. They were
somewhat scared of these
dogs and eventually passed
a law condemning most of
them to death, allowing each
shepherd just one dog to
guard his flocks. Known as
'verdinos' because of the
slightly green tinge to their
coats, the dogs had smooth
hair and broad jaws. They
were noted for their ferocity,
but also for their loyalty to
their owners. Today, as part
of the revived nationalism
of the *Canarios*, there is a
movement to keep the
verdino strain pure and have
it registered as a breed.

Barbary pirates and the fleets of Britain, Holland and Portugal frequently raided the islands. The most serious raid was carried out by the Dutch buccaneer, Pieter van der Does, who burnt down much of Las Palmas in 1599.

Boom and Bust

During the years of colonial rule, the Canary Islands in general – and Gran Canaria in particular – experienced turbulent economic fortunes. Reliance on various types of monoculture led to cycles of boom and bust, with downturns leading to mass emigrations to the New World. In the early 16th century, **sugar cane** was introduced to Gran Canaria from Asia. The industry was able to use slave labour and sugar became Gran Canaria's main source of income, along with the associated production of **rum**. The abolition of slavery in 1537, and the cheaper sugar produced in Brazil and central America, led to the collapse of the industry. The cultivation of sugar was replaced by the production of **wine**, but unfortunately Gran Canaria could not compete with Tenerife, which had more suitable soil for viticulture. The wine boom, however, ended early in the 19th century, because of competition from Madeira and diseases affecting the vines. This led to further emigration, mainly to Cuba and Venezuela.

In 1825, a new product was discovered. This was **cochineal** (a red dye), which was extracted from a small parasitic insect found on cactus plants. Thousands of prickly pear cactus plants soon appeared in many parts of Gran Canaria as this unusual type of farming boomed. By the 1870s more people chose to emigrate due to the emergence of chemical dyes and the decline in the cochineal trade.

Important political developments were taking place at this time. The Canary Islands were declared a province of Spain in 1821 and Santa Cruz de Tenerife was made the capital. Inter-island rivalry was prevalent between Gran Canaria and Tenerife, with Tenerife tending to dominate. Support for Gran Canaria, however, came with the rise to fame of **Fernando León y Castillo**. He was a native of the island who became the Foreign Minister of Spain and used his influence to increase the importance of the port of Las Palmas. A measure of political independence was established in 1912 when Spain introduced island councils or *cabildos*. In 1927 the Spanish government divided the Canary Islands into two provinces. The eastern province included Lanzarote, Fuerteventura and Gran Canaria, with its capital at Las Palmas, while the western province was made up of Tenerife and the smaller islands of La Gomera, El Hierro and La Palma, and the capital at Santa Cruz de Tenerife.

Opposite: *This old photograph of a family on Gran Canaria shows late 19th-century rural life.*
Below: *Prickly pear plants were introduced to Gran Canaria for the insect that produced the red cochineal dye.*

The Canary Islands' economy showed an upturn during the late 19th and early 20th centuries. This was influenced by their designation as a free trade zone and the growth of the Atlantic steamship trade. In the 1850s, British entrepreneurs introduced **banana and tomato farming** to the islands and by the turn of the century there were banana plantations in many areas of the wetter parts of Gran Canaria. Although bananas are still produced, the disruption caused by two world wars and the competition from Central and South America led to a decline in the market. The result of this was a further wave of emigration to the Americas. The extent of this is illustrated by the fact that over a quarter of a million people of Canary Island origin are estimated to live in Caracas, the capital of Venezuela.

The Rise of Franco

In the 1930s the Canary Islands found themselves involved in the Spanish Civil War. In March 1936

General Franco, who was suspected of planning a coup to overthrow the government, was exiled to Tenerife with the post of *Commandante-General*. Franco was in the Canary Islands for a mere four months, but during this time he survived three assassination attempts. He eventually fled to Morocco to lead the insurgents and began the brutal Civil War that was to divide towns and families.

The Growth of Tourism

Franco largely ignored the Canary Islands while he was in power in Spain, giving rise to an active separatist movement in the archipelago. The

Left: *Tourists taking dromedary rides in the southern part of the island.* **Opposite:** *Canary Island bananas are small and very tasty.*

movement was only stemmed in 1982, when the Canaries (and other parts of Spain) were given autonomous power and a regional constitution. After Franco died, **tourism** flourished in the Canaries, creating more jobs and thereby quelling the separatist movement. Tourism represents 80 per cent of Gran Canaria's income.

GOVERNMENT AND ECONOMY

The two provinces of the Canary Islands form one of the 17 autonomous regional communities in Spain. Rivalry between the islands is part of their history and the regional government has offices in both Santa Cruz de Tenerife and Las Palmas on Gran Canaria. The regional government has powers covering transport, agriculture, health and policing, and it also has the ability to raise local taxes. Each island has its own local administration known as the *cabildo,* while the lowest level of administration is the district or *municipio.*

The main **political parties** are the left wing Partido Socialista Obrero Español (PSOE) and the right of centre Partido Popular (PP). In the 1990s the various nationalist groups merged to form the Coalición Canaria (CC), which now – rather than pressing for independence – pushes Madrid for improvements. Most recent governments have been coalitions between the various parties.

EMIGRATION

Throughout the history of the Canary Islands, emigration has been a continuous activity, usually coinciding with downturns in the economy. Ships crossing the Atlantic frequently stopped to refuel in the Canary Islands and it was easy to book a passage or stow away. The usual destination was Latin America where Spanish was universally spoken. A favourite destination in the early years was Cuba, where emigrants from the Canaries played an important role in the growth of the capital, Havana, and also in the development of the cigar-making industry. During the difficult days of the Spanish Civil War, and later, World War II, there was renewed emigration, this time to Venezuela. However, since the growth of tourism, there has been plenty of work in the islands and there has been little need to emigrate. In fact, many northern Europeans are immigrants to the Canary Islands.

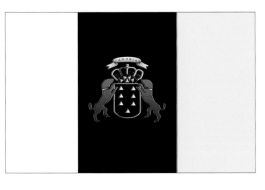

The Economy

Canarian **agriculture** has diversified over the years, as farmers have learnt that farming a single product is not profitable in the long run and most farms have a variety of enterprises. Crops include bananas, tomatoes, tobacco, coffee, citrus and exotic fruit and flowers. Animal husbandry is rare and confined to a few goats, sheep and cattle – cows are very rarely seen on Gran Canaria. The fertile volcanic soil, the equable climate and the use of plastic greenhouses and irrigation aid agricultural production. The growing spread of the use of plastic in agriculture is becoming a concern to environmentalists and does little to enhance the Gran Canarian scenery. The water supply has become a constant problem on the island, as precipitation levels have dropped (with the felling of forests) and the demands of tourism have increased. Much use is made of volcanic clinker to conserve soil moisture levels and more desalinisation plants are urgently required.

The **manufacturing industry** accounts for only 9 per cent of the island's GDP. Tax discounts are designed to attract business to the island and IVA (the Spanish equivalent of VAT) is only 4.5 per cent, compared to 16 per cent on the mainland. The **tertiary sector** (service sector) of industry is dominated by **tourism**. The Canary Islands are an all-year-round destination attracting over eight million visitors (recorded in 1998) annually. The tourists are mainly from Britain, Germany, Scandinavia, Holland and mainland Spain. This income has improved the islands' infrastructure, which benefits both the visitors and *Canarios*. Nevertheless, 16 per cent of the population is unemployed (although there is a sizeable 'grey economy', who according to statistics are unemployed, as they do not declare their earnings on tax returns) and average wages are amongst the lowest in the EU.

THE PEOPLE

The total **population** of the Canary Islands currently stands at 1,610,000 and grows at a rate of more than 1 per cent annually. The last census found that Gran Canaria has 770,000 inhabitants, which makes it the most populated island in the archipelago. Of this total, 365,000 live in the capital city, Las Palmas. These totals include a large number of foreign residents, mainly from Britain and Germany. There are also small numbers from the Americas, largely returning emigrants from countries such as Cuba and Venezuela. The people of Gran Canaria are mainly the descendants of Spaniards and are generally dark haired with an olive-skinned complexion. They are fiercely patriotic and regard themselves as *Canarios*, rather than from the *peninsular* (as they call mainland Spain). They have mixed feelings towards mainland Spaniards, who are sometimes called *godos* (or Goths), as they feel that they appropriate the local jobs. Indeed, many *Canarios* like to think of themselves as African rather than Spanish.

Like mainland Spaniards, *Canarios* are family-oriented. Machismo is still prevalent amongst certain communities,

> **UNFINISHED BUILDINGS**
>
> On the outskirts of many of the towns on Gran Canaria you will find numerous houses that have an unfinished look about them. This is often deliberate, as there is a massive tax levied on completed buildings. *Canarios* often prefer to have their homes unfinished than pay the tax, so they neglect to paint the walls or concrete a path in order to claim that the building is not yet complete.

Opposite: *The Canary Islands' regional flag, shown here, is raised alongside the Spanish flag on all official occasions.*
Below: *A plastic greenhouse used to aid tomato cultivation.*

but women have become increasingly liberated and now play a large role in public life, with many employed in the tourist industry.

Religion

The Spanish invaders brought **Roman Catholicism** with them to the Canary Islands and they swiftly converted the Guanches. It is still the official religion and it plays an important role in the lives of the people. Although weekly church attendance is not very high, most *Canarios* have church baptisms, weddings and funerals and attend church for various religious events noted on

Above: *A Canarian shepherd takes a rest from looking after his animals.*
Opposite: *Wayside shrines, such as this one near Puerto de Mogán, are a common feature in the Gran Canaria countryside.*

their calender. People from many parts of the world have settled in Gran Canaria and brought their religions with them. There is an **ecumenical church** holding multilingual services in the south of the island, a **mosque** in the Yumbo Centre (at Playa del Inglés) and there are also a few **synagogues**.

Festivals

Fiestas are the traditional way of celebrating saints' days on the religious calendar. These include the *Virgen del Pino*, the patron saint of Gran Canaria; *Corpus Christi*, when floral carpets are laid out on the streets; Easter (*Semana Santa*), which usually involves statues of the virgin being paraded through the streets; and the *Fiestas del Carmen*, marked by processions of boats. Some fiestas, like *La Bajada de la Rama* (a rain-making ritual in Agaete), are believed to go as far back as the Guanches. *Romerias* are processions led by decorated ox carts, which head from town churches to a hermitage (a place where a revered image is kept) or a similar location. There are many festivals of a secular nature, which may include a week long *feria* (fair). The *Carnaval* (Carnival) at Las Palmas may not be quite up to the standard of the one at Santa Cruz in Tenerife, but it ranks high by Spanish standards. Fireworks, bonfires, parades, traditional singing and folk dancing are an essential part of fiestas.

Sport and Recreation

The Canary Islands have some unique forms of sport that go back centuries and are enthusiastically followed by the locals. It is said that *Lucha Canaria* (Canarian wrestling) has its origins in Guanche trials of strength. Sand-covered arenas resembling bullrings are used for these wrestling competitions (bullfighting itself is not a popular sport in the Canary Islands).

The rules are strict; there are two teams, or 12 *luchadores* (participants), and two contestants at a time attempt to throw each other to the ground in a best of three *brega* (competition) – only the soles of the feet may touch the ground. Canarian wrestling is not a violent sport, as punching and kicking are not allowed, and skill and balance are more important than weight and size. The team that wins the most *bregas* claims the overall match. *Luchas* are often held at the original Guanche locations over fiestas. *Juego del Palo* (stick fighting) also originated in preconquest days. It is a contest using 2m (6.6ft) wooden staves called *banot* with which the contestants aim to do the maximum damage to each other. Even longer staves of around 2.5m (8.2ft) are used

THE VIRGEN DEL CARMEN FESTIVAL

The Virgen del Carmen is the patron saint of fishermen and seafarers. Each July the fishing villages around the coast of Gran Canaria celebrate this saint with a spectacular festival. The image of the virgin is taken from the parish church and paraded around the streets, ending up at the beach or harbour. Here she is briefly taken into the sea either on the shoulders of the fishermen or on a boat, before being taken back to her sanctuary. Singing, dancing, fireworks and the cooking of giant paellas accompany the fiesta.

MEAT ON THE MENU

Cattle and sheep are rarely seen on the island and pigs are usually kept in barns. The only domestic farm animals likely to be spotted are herds of goats. It is surprising, therefore, to find that meat is common on restaurant menus. Beef (*carne de vaca*) is actually imported from South America, while pork (*cerdo*) and lamb (*cordero*) are local products. Kid (*cabrito*) is a local favourite, but quite expensive. Rabbit (*conejo*) is usually served with a spicy garlic and chilli (*mojo*) sauce.

Opposite: Papas arrugadas *are small potatoes boiled in salty water.*
Below: *Water sports are very popular on the island.*

in the *Salto del Regaton de la Garrocha*, a form of pole vaulting in which contestants leap down a mountainside and across deep ravines. Less appealing to tourists will be **cock fighting**, which has a strong following in Gran Canaria.

The more international spectator sports are also extremely popular in the Canary Islands. As in the rest of Spain, **football** is obsessively followed. UD Las Palmas are in the Spanish Second Division and their local derbies against rival Club Deportivo Tenerife are amongst the highlights of the Canary Islands' sporting year. Other important sports include **beach volleyball**, **tennis** and **golf**. The Atlantic Ocean offers many possibilities for **water sports**, for locals and tourists alike. **Sailing**, **waterskiing**, **windsurfing** and **power-boat racing** are all highly popular. The clear and warm waters of the Atlantic are perfect for **scuba diving** and **snorkelling** and there are a number of undersea national parks around the shores of the islands. The ocean also provides ideal conditions for **game fishing**. Charter boats are available for swordfish, tunny, shark and marlin fishing.

Food and Drink

The **food** of Gran Canaria illustrates a wide range of influences from other countries, including mainland Spain, northern Europe and even the Americas. Typical Canarian food is most likely to be found in the capital, Las Palmas and in the more rural areas rather than in the main resorts, where restaurants tend to serve international food. If the visitor wishes to sample true Canarian food then the unusual meal times in Gran Canaria must be appreciated. **Breakfast** (*desayuno*) is generally light and rarely served before 09:30. It usually consists of coffee, a sandwich (*bocadillo*) or a small cake (*pastel*). **Lunch** (*almuerzo*) is usually eaten after 14:30 and may have been preceded by *tapas*, which are light snacks served at the bar. Lunch, for many *Canarios*, is the main meal of the day and **dinner** (*cena*) is a lighter meal, which is usually eaten after 22:00.

There are two fares in Gran Canaria that the visitor should certainly sample. One is *gofio* (ground and toasted wheat or maize), the island's traditional staple food which goes back to Guanche times. The other is *papas arrugadas*, small new potatoes with wrinkly skins, which are boiled in very salty water and served with most main courses.

GOFIO

This is one of the few culinary items to have survived from Guanche times. *Gofio* was once made from the glasswort plant, but after the Spanish introduced Indian corn, this became the main ingredient. It is mixed with wheat flour, toasted (or roasted) and then used in a variety of ways. It can be sprinkled on food or used to thicken stews or soups. *Gofio* can also be made into a breakfast cereal or mixed with figs or almonds to make a dessert. Unfortunately, few visitors to Gran Canaria get the opportunity to try *gofio*, as it is rarely on the menu in the main tourist resorts. Those who are keen to try this Canarian staple food will need to drive into the interior and find a rural restaurant with *gofio* on the menu.

Main meals on Gran Canaria are usually introduced with a starter, such as a salad (*ensalada*) or a soup (*sopa*) – watercress soup (*potaje de berros*) is a speciality and other favourites are fish soup (*sopa de pescada*) and vegetable soup (*sopa de verdura*). Most restaurants also offer the popular mainland cold soup, *gazpacho*, which consists of finely chopped onions, tomatoes and garlic. The main course usually includes meat (*carne*) or fish (*pescado*). The most commonly offered meats are beef (*ternera*), chicken (*pollo*), lamb (*cordero*), pork (*cerdo*) and rabbit (*conejo*). The prolific wild rabbits are hunted on the island and some are domestically reared for the table. The meat may be grilled (*à la parilla*), roasted (*asado*) or it may be prepared in a stew (*estafado* or *puchero*). A mouth-watering variety of fish and shellfish are also found on menus. Fish is usually prepared simply, either fried (*frito*) or grilled (*à la plancha*). At some of the better fish restaurants, it is possible to choose your own fish from a tank or display refrigerator. The price is subject to the weight of the fish. The most common fish on the menu are sea bass (*cherne*), hake (*merluza*), swordfish (*pez espada*), sole (*lenguado*), tuna (*atun* or *bonito*), and parrot fish (*vieja*). Some excellent shellfish is also available, including prawns (*gambas*), mussels (*mejiones*) and squid (*calamares*). Particular Gran Canarian specialities are the sauces provided with both the fish and meat dishes. The red *mojo rojo* is a spicy vinaigrette-type sauce made from a mixture of chilli, cumin, paprika and saffron and usually served with meat or *papas arrugadas*. *Mojo verde* is a green variation with coriander or parsley instead of paprika, a perfect accompaniment to fish. Vegetables are rather limited, but you can always ask for food to suite your needs or eat *tapas*.

The choice of **desserts** (*postres*) is usually confined to Spanish favourites such as crème caramel (*flan*), a honey and almond dessert (*bienmesabe*), ice cream (*helado*), fruit (*fruta*) or nougat (*turrón*). Local cheese on offer is white goats-milk cheese (*queso blanco*) or *queso de flor*, a mixture of cow and sheep's milk flavoured with the flowers of a thistle.

The main resort areas in the south of Gran Canaria also offer a bewildering variety of foreign restaurants. Chinese and Indian restaurants are particularly common, but many other nationalities are also represented. English breakfasts are offered in many places. Visitors on a budget should try the menu of the day (*menu del día*), which usually offers a starter, a main course and a dessert, as well as bread and a drink, for a bargain price.

Sampling **alcoholic drinks** is popular amongst holidaymakers and Gran Canaria offers plenty of choice, including

Opposite: *Rabbit, or* conejo, *often cooked with garlic, is a popular meat dish.*
Below: *Restaurants, such as this one in Puerto Rico, often cater expressly for British needs.*

some local specialities, at reasonable prices. Some **wine** is produced in Gran Canaria, mainly in the area around El Monte, but the island does not provide the quality or quantity of neighbouring Tenerife. Most wines offered at restaurants, therefore, are from the Spanish mainland. There are some popular wine-based summer drinks, including *tinto de verano* (a mixture of wine and lemon-ade) and the deceptively strong *sangria*, which is a combination of red wine, lemonade and liqueurs, gar-nished with fruit and ice. The local **beer** in Gran Canaria is the easily drinkable *Tropical*, while *Dorada*, made on Tenerife, is also available along with numerous foreign brews. For a small draught beer, ask for *una caña*. Amongst the spirits are mainland brandies (*coñac*), such as *Fundador* and *Sobrerano*. The best known Gran Canarian spirit is rum (*ron*), which is made near Arucas from locally grown sugar cane. Another variety is *ron miel*, a rum liqueur with added honey. There are a number of other **liqueurs**, many of which are made from the subtropical fruits grown on Gran Canaria. The most popular is *Cobana*, a yellow banana liqueur that comes in a striking bottle. Remember that spirit measures (if they are used at all) are two or three times larger than you would expect at home!

The most popular of the **non-alcoholic drinks** is coffee, which comes in a variety of forms. Any bar with a good reputation will make their coffee in an espresso machine and for an espresso-type coffee ask either for a *cafe solo* (which is black) or *cafe cortado* (which has just a drop of milk). *Cafe con leche* is milky coffee. Don't be

Opposite: *Miniature figures in local costume are a popular purchase with tourists.*
Below: Tropical *is a favoured variety of local Canary Island beer.*

surprised if your coffee arrives in a glass. *Canarios* often take a shot of rum in their coffee or have an accompanying *coñac* (the Spanish equivalent of the French cognac). Tea is also available, but usually served rather weak. A chocolate drink is popular with breakfast for Gran Canarios, who often dunk their *churros* (a form of doughnut) into the beverage. There is a full range of soft drinks (*refrescos*) and fruit juices (*zumos*) available.

Crafts

Tourists find a wide variety of craft goods to take home as souvenirs. The production of craft articles is a major source of income for many of the rural villages of Gran Canaria. Sadly, however, many of the items on sale in souvenir shops are cheap imitations from abroad and this is a considerable threat to the survival of ancient craft skills on the island. Many of the handicrafts that are so admired by tourists were once essential to the daily way of life in past centuries.

Fine **woodwork** can be seen in the ornately carved balconies, in the older towns of Gran Canaria, and on furniture and cedarwood chests. **Basketwork**, using wood, cane straw as well as palm and banana leaves, is a common craft throughout the island with the main

WOODEN BALCONIES

Wood carving has been practiced for a very long time on the Canary Islands, both in craft work and in the Plateresque-style carvings (*see* page 35) found in church interiors dating from the 16th and 17th centuries. With plenty of Canary pine available it was inevitable that the style would influence domestic architecture. The pine is easily carved, but also very durable, and fine examples are the intricately carved balconies of the mansions in the older parts of Las Palmas, such as Vegueta, and in some of the older towns in the north of the island, such as Teror and Telde.

SAN ANTONIO MARIA CLARET
MISIONERO EN SAN MATEO
FEBRERO 1849-1999
150 ANIVERSARIO

Above: *The production of ceramic tiles, such as these in an impression of San Mateo, is an important craft industry.*

Opposite: *There are numerous caves on Gran Canaria. Once lived in by the Guanches, many are now used as agricultural stores.*

centre being Teror. Examples include straw hats, fans, baskets and bags. The craft of pottery has its beginnings in Guanche times and it is still made in the traditional way – without using a wheel. The main centres of production are Arucas, Atalya and Santa Brígida. The pots vary in size – from large urns in which olive oil was stored, down to small vases and ashtrays. Look out for the small *Idolos de Tara* (Guanche-style figurines) and the *pinterderas* (clay seals with an imprint or design), which were probably used as brooches. The Guía area is famous for its **bone** knives, which were originally used by men working in banana fields. You will also find brooches and earrings made from bone. Probably the most attractive souvenirs (and the lightest to carry home) are the **textiles**. Exquisitely embroidered cloth is seen in the colourful national costumes that are worn at local festivals. Tablecloths, napkins and handkerchiefs are the most commonly displayed items, but these are also the craft goods that are most often brought in from abroad. Look for the genuine articles at the artisan shops. Traditional **musical instruments** can also be bought, including the *timple* (a five-stringed ukelele) and the *chácaras* (large castanets). Other interesting craft souvenirs include **rag dolls** in national costume, items made from polished **volcanic stone** and **lacework** made by the island's nuns.

The Arts

Although the Guanches left numerous examples of wall paintings in caves, it took some time before any notable Canary Island **painters** emerged. Most of the 17th-, 18th- and 19th-century painters confined their work to religious themes and some of their paintings may be seen in the churches on the island. Perhaps Gran Canaria's best-known artist was Néstor de la Torre (1887–1938), who specialized in murals and was responsible for a campaign to revive Canarian folk art and architecture. His work can be seen in the Museo Néstor in the Pueblo Canario in Las Palmas. The work of the versatile César Manrique – artist, architect and environmentalist – can be seen throughout the Canary Islands, particularly in the design of outdoor pool complexes.

José Luján Pérez (1756–1815) was a renowned **sculptor** and his work can be found in churches and cathedrals throughout the Canary Islands. Although the Guanches had no written language, **literature** has a long history in the Canary Islands. Indeed, there is a well known saying that 'the Canaries is a land of poets'. There have been many novelists and poets over the centuries, but most of them have had to move to the mainland to gain recognition for their work. Gran Canaria's best known novelist is Benito Pérez Galdós (1843–1920), whose house in the Triana district of Las Palmas is now a museum.

There are some fine **museums** and **art galleries** in the Canary Islands. On Gran Canaria, most of the best museums are in Las Palmas. Try to visit the **Casa de Colón** for Columbus memorabilia, the **Centro Atlántico de Arte Moderno** for modern art and the **Museo Canario** for a glimpse of the Stone Age Guanche way of life.

> **THE UNUSUAL *TIMPLE***
>
> On the island of Gran Canaria, most traditional dancing and songs are accompanied by the *timple* (pronounced tim-play). It is a stringed instrument closely akin to the ukulele and the mandolin. It is made of wood and has a rounded back. It normally has five strings, although there is a four-stringed version called the *contra*, which is found on Lanzarote. Once thought to have originated from the Spanish *guitarillo*, it is now believed that Berber slaves brought it to the islands. The *timple* is played at all the local fiestas. It was even exported to Latin American countries with the many waves of emigrants and it is a predominant instrument in Cuban and Venezuelan folk music. The souvenir shops at Gran Canaria's Gando airport sell CDs featuring *timple* music and they are a fitting memento of a holiday on the island.

Music and Dance

Although the Canary Islands have not produced any well-known composers, classical music is taken seriously and concerts are always well supported. Traditional folk music and dancing are always observed during fiesta times. Dances include the lively *isa* and the more dignified *folia*. Occasionally the *tajaraste*, a dance believed to have its origins in Guanche times, may be performed. Traditional instruments, such as the *chácaras* and the *timple*, accompany the dancing. Immigrants have introduced many dances, such as the *malagueña* and the *sevillaña* from Andalucía. Popular music includes Latin American *salsa* rhythms.

Architecture

The Guanches, who were largely cave dwellers, left little legacy in the way of vernacular architecture. The oldest buildings in Gran Canaria date back to the Spanish

Conquest. Since this time, no destructive wars have occurred and because of this and the mild weather, many of the island's ancient buildings are well preserved. The Gothic style was on its way out at the time of the conquest and many of the early buildings were constructed in the **Mudéjar** style, which is a blend of both Gothic and Islamic style developed by Christians after the 15th-century *reconquista* of Spain. The *Mudéjar* style encompasses the need for water and protection from the sun. Most houses are built around a central courtyard or *patio*, often with a decorated well. In the larger houses, the *patio* had shady trees and a colonnaded cloister. This scheme was also common on the front of the house, with a columned, covered walkway at ground level and a balcony on the first floor. The balconies were made of wood and often elaborately decorated. There are some superb examples of this colonial style in the old parts of Teror and Telde. Artisans' houses from this period are much simpler stone and whitewashed buildings, with flat roofs in the drier south of the island and tiled roofs in the wetter parts. There is a simple way to date the houses in Gran Canaria – up to the end of the 17th century, windows were often placed at irregular levels, but since then house façades have become symmetrical, with a door at the centre and equal-sized windows.

A number of other architectural styles can be seen in Gran Canaria. By the 16th century, the *Mudéjar* style had been replaced by the intricate **Plateresque**, named after the work of silversmiths and particularly evident in some carved ceilings. By the 19th century, **Portuguese Baroque** had appeared, typified by iron railings on balconies. During the same period public buildings, such as town halls and museums, were constructed in the **Neoclassical** style. The early 20th century saw some interesting **Art Nouveau** buildings, which were mainly the work of César Manrique. The second half of the century brought the growth of tourism and with it came some unattractive, multi-storeyed apartment blocks. The more recent tourist developments are of a low-rise variety and are designed with the environment in mind.

Opposite Top: *Ornate metalwork on this old wooden door.*
Opposite Bottom: *Colourful tiles, or* azulejos, *are a common feature of domestic architecture.*
Below: *The symmetrical pattern of this house in Las Palmas dates it as post-17th century.*

APPRECIATING GRAN CANARIA'S CHURCHES

The only cathedral on the Canary Islands is in Gran Canaria, which also has a fine selection of churches to visit. Many churches date from the early 16th century and display a variety of styles. Few are genuinely **Gothic**, but there are many examples of the *Mudéjar* style, which had its origins in the Moorish occupation of southern Spain. Other churches display the ornate **Plateresque** decoration. Also, look for some beautifully carved wooden ceilings. Stained glass windows are generally uninspiring, but this is more than compensated for by the superb interior decoration. The altar screens (*retablos*) are often highly carved and dripping with gold leaf. Many churches have carvings by José Luján Pérez (1756–1815), the greatest of Canarian sculptors. When visiting Gran Canaria's churches, remember that beachwear is inappropriate and not appreciated by the locals.

2
Las Palmas de Gran Canaria

The capital of the eastern province of the Canary Islands, Las Palmas, is the only settlement in the archipelago that has the atmosphere of a big city. Although unmistakably Spanish, the city has an international quality with tourists mingling with sailors from container ships, both searching for bargains in the Indian-run bazaars. Amongst the population of over 350,000 are people from all over the world who have chosen to settle here either for work or retirement, as well as many returning emigrants from Latin America. The immense size of Las Palmas brings added problems to the city. Traffic jams are frequent and trying to find a parking space is almost impossible. It is also the only city in the islands where precautions need to be taken against street crime. But don't be deterred – there is much of interest in Las Palmas and a day trip to the city should be on the itinerary of any visitor to Gran Canaria.

Las Palmas lies in the northeast corner of Gran Canaria and spreads along 14km (8 miles) of the coastline. There is a sizable historic quarter, based in the districts of **Vegueta** and **Triana** where the cathedral and a clutch of good museums are found. Further north is the **Cuidad Jardín**, a garden city area laid out by the British, and the **Pueblo Canario**, which is a modern Spanish equivalent. Las Palmas is a shopper's delight with covered markets and bazaars, where bargaining is encouraged, as well as a branch of El Corte Inglés, Spain's premier department store. In the far north of Las Palmas, in the **Santa Catalina** district, the land narrows

Don't Miss

*** Museo Canario: explore the Canary Islands' foremost museum.
*** Casa de Colón: Christopher Columbus memorabilia in the former governor's house.
*** Catedral de Santa Ana: Gran Canaria's only cathedral in Vegueta.
** Playa de las Canteras: enjoy the popular and crowded city beach backed by hotels and restaurants.
* Parque de Santa Catalina: this vibrant square is the heart of the city.

Opposite: *Pavement cafes spill out onto this attractive square in the capital.*

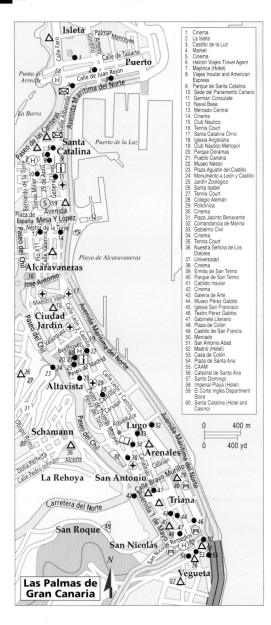

Las Palmas de Gran Canaria

1. Cinema
2. La Isleta
3. Castillo de la Luz
4. Market
5. Cinema
6. Halcón Viajes Travel Agent
7. Majórica (Hotel)
8. Viajes Insular and American Express
9. Parque de Santa Catalina
10. Sede del Parlamento Canario
11. German Consulate
12. Naval Base
13. Mercado Central
14. Cinema
15. Club Nautico
16. Tennis Court
17. Santa Catalina Clinic
18. Iglesia Anglicana
19. Club Náutico Metropol
20. Parque Doramas
21. Pueblo Canaria
22. Museo Néstor
23. Plaza Agustin del Castillo
24. Monumento a León y Castillo
25. Jardín Zoológico
26. Santa Isabel
27. Tennis Court
28. Colegio Alemán
29. Policlinica
30. Cinema
31. Plaza Jacinto Benavente
32. Comandancia de Marina
33. Gobierno Civil
34. Cinema
35. Tennis Court
36. Nuestra Señora de Los Dolores
37. Universidad
38. Cinema
39. Ermita de San Telmo
40. Parque de San Telmo
41. Cabildo Insular
42. Cinema
43. Galeria de Arte
44. Museo Pérez Galdós
45. Iglesia San Francisco
46. Teatro Pérez Galdós
47. Gabinete Literario
48. Plaza de Colón
49. Castillo de San Francis
50. Mercado
51. San Antonio Abad
52. Madrid (Hotel)
53. Casa de Colón
54. Plaza de Santa Ana
55. CAAM
56. Catedral de Santa Ana
57. Santo Domingo
58. Imperial Playa (Hotel)
59. El Corte Ingles Department Store
60. Santa Catalina (Hotel and Casino)

0   400 m

0   400 yd

to an isthmus, linking the city with the former island of **La Isleta**. Each side of the isthmus is in contrast to the other. On the west are the golden sands of the **Playa de las Canteras**, backed by hotels, apartment blocks and a number of restaurants, while on the east there is the harbour of **Puerto de la Luz**, one of the busiest ports in Spain.

HISTORY

There were most certainly Guanches in the area when the first serious European conquistador, Juán Rejón, arrived in 1477 and this date marks the effective start of the city's history. The invaders named their landing spot **Real de las Palmas** and it quickly became an important military camp in the campaign to overpower the local population. Las Palmas became a cathedral city in 1485, with the bishopric being transferred from Lanzarote. The port grew quickly as trade with the Latin American countries developed, but a disadvantage of this growth was the fact that Las Palmas became a favourite target for pirates from all the

seafaring nations. Drake and Hawkins, amongst others, made raids on Las Palmas, but it was the Dutchman Pieter van der Does, who in 1599, made the most damaging attack, burning down much of the town.

The fortunes of Las Palmas reflected the agricultural 'boom and bust' cycles of the 18th and 19th centuries. Fortunately, the city seemed to bounce back each time, with the assistance of British entrepreneurs and trading families who introduced new crops and also arranged for the city's water, electricity and mains drainage to be installed.

The port of Las Palmas developed as a supply stop for transatlantic sailing vessels and, later, when steamships came about, the harbour provided coal. A further boost was welcomed when a native of the city, **Fernando León y Castillo**, became the foreign minister of Spain and was able to sponsor major developments for the port. The growth of Las Palmas eventually forced the Spanish government to divide the Canary Islands into two provinces in 1927. Las Palmas became the capital of the eastern province, which consisted of Gran Canaria, Lanzarote and Fuerteventura.

In 1936, General Franco launched a coup from Las Palmas, which was to begin the Spanish Civil War. World War II followed and for two decades Las Palmas was in decline as its shipping trade was severely disrupted. The recovery period was slow, but it was assisted by the development of the tourist trade in the 1960s. Las Palmas was initially the main holiday resort on the

Above: *An alluring view of the coastline of Las Palmas, Spain's seventh largest city.*

STREET SAFETY

Las Palmas is probably the only city in the Canary Islands where street crime is a problem, but it is only found in a small part of the city. Most visitors to Las Palmas do not experience any difficulties at all, but it is wise to take a few sensible precautions. Look out for pickpockets in crowded places such as markets and bus stations. Avoid ill-lit areas late at night, particularly near the port and in the red light district north of Parque de Santa Catalina. Leave all valuables in the hotel safe and carry cash and credit cards in a body pouch. Do not leave any valuables on display in cars.

Right: *The Catedral de Santa Ana, whose tree-lined plaza is the home of hundreds of pigeons.*

island, but the focus of the industry later shifted to the south of Gran Canaria, where resorts such as Playa del Inglés took advantage of the more reliable climate. Today, Las Palmas is the main city and port of the Canary Islands, with a thriving service industry and a population of over 350,000 people. The Historic Quarter of Las Palmas is in the south and consists of the districts of **Vegueta** and **Triana**, separated by a busy highway.

VEGUETA

A stroll around the historic quarter of Vegueta is an essential part of a visit to Las Palmas. Narrow cobbled streets lead to small squares, and the surrounding buildings are decorated with carved stonework, ornate iron lamps, grilled windows and traditional Canarian wooden balconies. A glimpse through a doorway may reveal a shady patio with a fountain and flower-bedecked walls.

Catedral de Santa Ana ★★★

Dominating the area is the **Catedral de Santa Ana**. The construction of the cathedral began in 1497, just 10 years after the arrival of the first conquistador, but it was not until the 19th century that it was finally completed. Not surprisingly, it shows a variety of architectural styles. The neoclassical west front was designed by the local sculptor and architect, José Luján Pérez (1756–1815), and was completed in the 19th century. Inside the cathedral

---

TALENTED BROTHERS

During the 20th century, Las Palmas was fortunate to have had amongst its residents two highly talented brothers. **Miguel Martin Fernández de la Torre** was an architect and builder and was responsible for the construction of the Teatro Pérez Galdós and the Pueblo Canario. His brother **Néstor Martin Férnandez de la Torre** was the first artist from the Canary Islands to have gained international recognition. He was an exponent of the modernisme style of painting and was involved in a number of interior designs, including the painting of the Teatro Pérez Galdós. A good collection of his work can be viewed in the Museo Néstor in the Pueblo Canario.

elements of Gothic and Plateresque styles can be observed amongst the three naves, numerous chapels and cupolas. Interesting pieces are the unusual bishop's throne, statues by Pérez and the impressive *retablo* (a highly decorated screen) behind the high altar, which came from Cataluña in mainland Spain. At the side of the cathedral, entered via Calle Espíritu Santo, is the **Museo Diocesano de Arte Sacro** (Diocesan Museum of Sacred Art). Apart from the usual church treasures, there is a fascinating collection of art from former Spanish colonies as well as some Aztec items. Wander out into the courtyard; the **Patio de las Naranjos**, with its oranges trees and fountain, is reminiscent of Moorish Andalucía. Both the museum and the cathedral are open from Monday to Friday (09:00–13:30 and 16:00–18:30) and the museum has an admission charge.

Plaza de Santa Ana ★

Opposite the west front of the cathedral is the small oblong **Plaza de Santa Ana**, which is guarded by bronze statues of dogs – the city's heraldic emblem. On the right-hand side of the square is the **Palacio Episcopal** (also known as the Bishop's Palace), dating from ca. 1630, which is, unfortunately, not open to the public. Just next to it is the **Casa Regental**, which once housed the leaders of the island's armed forces. It is now occupied by the city's law courts. At the far end of Plaza de Santa Ana, facing the cathedral, is the *ayuntamiento* (the town

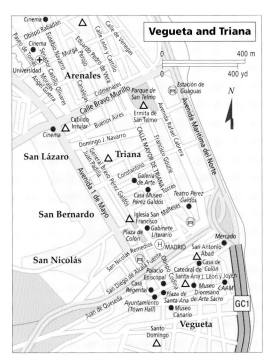

CLIMATE

Las Palmas is in the northern, wetter part of Gran Canaria, but the lack of mountains in the immediate vicinity results in a low annual rainfall. Light rain is experienced throughout the year, except in June, July and August. Try to avoid these months, as the city is crowded and hot. Winter temperatures are very pleasant – it is rarely cold in Las Palmas, but it can be windy.

Vegueta and Triana

GUANCHE MUMMIFICATION

The **Museo Canario** offers the opportunity to see Guanche **mummies**. The Guanches mummified their corpses in a similar, but cruder way to the ancient Egyptians. It appears that only the bodies belonging to members of the higher echelons of society were treated in this way. Intestines were removed from the bodies, which were then soaked in goat's milk and wrapped with reeds and animal skins. The bodies were then left to dry in the sun for around 14 days. This rather unpleasant work was carried out by lower caste Guanches, who tended to be ostracized by their society. The bodies were placed in remote, inaccessible caves and it is for this reason that mummies are still being discovered today. It appears that the mummified chiefs or *guanatemes* were laid in wooden boxes and then placed upright against the cave walls.

hall). This, surprisingly, is the youngest building in the square, as its predecessor was burnt down after it was struck by a firework during a fiesta in 1842. Other buildings include the **Historical Archives Office** and the house of the writer Jose Vieram y Clavijo. The best time to see the square is during Corpus Christi, when it is covered with a carpet of flowers (*see* panel on page 43).

Museo Canario ★★★

Just two blocks away from the cathedral, in Calle Doctor Chil, is the **Museo Canario** (the street is named after the anthropologist who founded the museum in the 19th century). This, undoubtedly the finest museum in the Canary Islands, is devoted to the inhabitants of the archipelago before Spanish times. There is a comprehensive collection of Guanche artefacts, including pottery, agricultural implements, seals and jewellery. More macabre exhibits, such as the world's largest collection of Cro-Magnon skulls, are also on display. The skulls were all collected locally and have given rise to arguments concerning the origins of the Guanches. There are also a number of Guanche mummies, with detailed explanations on the way they were preserved. Don't miss the accurate mock up of the Cueva Pintada, since the actual Painted Cave near Gáldar is closed to the public. The privately owned Museo Canario is open from Monday to Friday (10:00–17:00), and on Saturday (10:00–13:00) and Sunday (10:00–14:00). There is an admission charge.

Opposite: *The Casa de Colón where Columbus may have briefly stayed. It has some fine wooden balconies and stonework.*
Right: *Displays at the Museo Canario, where numerous Guanche mummies can be seen.*

Casa de Colón ★★★

Another museum in Vegueta, that is particularly popular with coach parties, is the **Casa de Colón** (the House of Christopher Columbus). It is claimed that Columbus stayed in this house on his first voyage of discovery in 1492, while waiting for a rudder to be repaired. This is debatable, but whatever the truth, the museum is well worth a visit. The exterior of the building is superb, with a fine stone Plateresque doorway facing a small square with a fountain, plus numerous wooden balconies in traditional Canarian style. It was a fitting home for many of the island's early governors. Inside, there is a beautiful covered patio, complete with a well and guarded by some noisy parrots. The rooms contain Columbus memorabilia, including charts, models of the *Niña*, the *Pinta*, the *Santa María*, weapons and other nautical artefacts. There is a realistic reconstruction of the poop deck of the *Niña* in another room and a small art gallery with some paintings on loan from the Prado in Madrid. Entrance to the Casa de Colón is free and it is open from Monday to Friday (09:00–18:00) and on Saturday and Sunday (09:00–15:00). Nearby, in a cobbled courtyard at the end of Calle Colón, is the small chapel of **San Antonio Abad**. Here, it is claimed, Columbus prayed on the night before he set sail for the Americas. If true, Columbus would certainly not recognise it today, as it was completely rebuilt in 1892.

FLOWER CARPETS

Try to be in Las Palmas for the **Corpus Christi festival** (usually in late May or early June). In mainland Spain, scattering flowers on the pavements celebrates this special festival on the religious calendar, and it has also become a fine event in various parts of the Canary Islands. In Tenerife, both flowers and volcanic soil are used to decorate the occasion, but in Gran Canaria flowers alone are used. The adorning designs are geometric, floral and depict scenes from the Bible. In Las Palmas, the best place to see floral carpets is in the Plaza Santa Ana, just opposite the town's cathedral.

GUANCHE SKULL PIERCING

In the Museo Canario in Las Palmas there are scores of skulls dating back to Guanche times. Many of them show the drilled holes that were typical of the Guanches. In the medical world the process, carried out with metal drills, is known as trepanning and it was a common practice in the 14th century. The Guanches, however, had no knowledge of metals, so they must have used stone – probably the glassy volcanic rock known as obsidian.

Right: *The shady plazas of Las Palmas are perfect places to relax and catch up with the news.*
Opposite: *A tour around the historic sites by horse and carriage (*coche de caballos) *is a sedate way of seeing the city.*

Centro Atlántico de Arte Moderno *

Visitors interested in art will certainly wish to visit the **Centro Atlántico de Arte Moderno (CAAM)**, located in Vegueta's most attractive street, the Calle de Balcones. Behind the building's 18th century façade is a modern five-storey structure containing paintings by contemporary Spanish and Canarian artists. There is no admission charge at the CAAM and it is open from Tuesday to Saturday (10:00–21:00) and on Sunday (10:00–14:00).

The Market *

One other place worth a visit in Vegueta is the *Mercado* (market), which is located in the northeast corner of the district next to the coastal motorway. Known to the locals as the 'Market of the Forty Thieves', it sells fruit, vegetables, fish, meat and handicrafts, providing an authentic slice of Canarian life. There are excellent food outlets around the market, including a number of good *tapas* bars.

TRIANA

Triana is almost as old as Vegueta, but it is far busier and somewhat more commercialized. Its name is taken from the gypsy quarter of the same name in Sevilla, mainland Spain, from where most of the immigrants who have settled here originated.

COLUMBUS IN LAS PALMAS?

Las Palmas is rich in associations with Christopher Columbus (or Cristóbal Colón as he is known in Spain). There is the **Casa de Colón**, where he is supposed to have stayed while his ship was being repaired. Nearby is the **Chapel of San Antonio Abad**, where the explorer is said to have prayed before setting out to the Americas. There is also the **Plaza de Colón**, with an imposing bust of the mariner. Recent historical evidence, however, suggests that Columbus never set foot on Gran Canaria and, in 1992, the island did not take part in the 500th-anniversary celebrations concerning the explorer's discoveries.

Triana is separated from Vegueta by a dried-up river valley, which is now occupied by the dual carriageway that leads southwest to Santa Brígida and other commuter towns. The **Parque de San Telmo** marks the northern edge of Triana and this shady square, unfortunately a spot frequented by alcoholics, is noted for its restored modernist kiosk with its colourful tiles. In the western corner of the park is the **Ermita de San Telmo**, a small Baroque-style chapel named after the patron saint of fishermen. It was rebuilt in the 17th century after being partly destroyed by Van de Does and his pirates. Don't miss the particularly fine *artesonado* (panelled) ceiling. This area was also the site of Las Palmas's first jetty jutting out into the Atlantic. Alongside the square you can see the barracks from which Franco instigated his *coup d'etat* in 1936 that lead to the Spanish Civil War. On the opposite side of the square is the city's bus station, the **Estación de Guaguas**, where buses that provide transport around the north of the island and to and from the airport are based.

Cutting through Triana from north to south is the main shopping street, the **Calle Mayor de Triana**. This

BOTE RACING

During the 19th century ships were serviced in Las Palmas harbour by small craft called *botes*. They had both oars and sails and spent their time ferrying people and supplies from ship to shore. During quiet periods the *botes* would race each other around the harbour and along the shore. These eventually developed into formal regattas and the custom continues today. There are nearly 20 of these craft left and they race regularly over weekends during the summer months. Each *bote*, which meets a standard of particular measurements, represents a different district of the city.

VEGETARIANS

Vegetarians who intend eating out during their stay, may find that it is difficult to satisfy their dietary requirements. At restaurants, an *ensalada mixta* (salad) can be ordered as starter, but this will often include tuna or chorizo sausages. Main courses of meat or fish are usually accompanied by a token garnishing of salad, as well as *papas fritas* (chips) or *papas arrugadas* (new potatoes boiled in heavily salted water), but rarely vegetables. It is always possible to ask your waiter for something that will suit your dietery needs. There are plenty of fresh vegetables available on the island, so vegetarians might also find it convenient to self-cater.

traffic-free street is full of fashionable shops and it is a favourite venue for the locals to take their evening stroll (*paseo*). The Calle Mayor de Triana is also notable for its fine and varied domestic architecture, with *modernisme* (the Spanish version of art nouveau) much to the fore. Shop façades are not allowed to be obtrusive – even McDonalds blends in with its setting.

The Columbus theme is continued just to the west of the Calle Mayor in the **Plaza de Colón**, where there is a bust of the explorer. Also in this square is Triana's oldest church, the **Iglesia San Francisco**. It has gradually been restored since the fires of 1599. Fortunately, the *Mudéjar* ceiling remains in a good state. Look out for the Virgen de la Soledad – her facial features are said to resemble Isabella I.

At the southern end of the Calle Mayor de Triana is the sombre bulk of the **Teatro Pérez Galdós**, named after the novelist who was a native of Las Palmas. The theatre, which opened in 1919, was designed by Miguel Martín de la Torre, who arranged for his brother Nestor to paint the interior murals (*see* page 40). Their erotic themes shocked the local theatregoers! Outside the theatre is a statue of the French composer Charles Camille Saint-Saëns (1835–1921) who lived on Gran Canaria for a while. Fans of Galdós can also visit his birthplace, **Casa Museo Pérez Galdós**, at Calle Cano 6. The building is of considerable interest, being an attractive townhouse with a lovely courtyard. Inside are many of the author's personal possessions, including manuscripts, letters, books and photographs of actors who performed his works. There is also a rather

Left: *Local buses provide a cheap service from Las Palmas to all parts of the island.*
Opposite: *Salad is commonly offered as a starter, but vegetables rarely accompany main courses.*

grotesque wax model of Galdós sitting at his desk. The house is open from Monday to Friday (09:00–13:00 and 16:00–20:00) and admission is free.

THE CENTRAL AREA OF LAS PALMAS

Immediately north of Triana are the rather scruffy inner city residential districts of **Arenales** and **Lugo**, which are of little interest to the tourist. Bypass these by taking the No.1 bus northwards from the Estación de Guaguas and alighting at **Parque Doramas**, which was named after a Guanche chief who died resisting the Spaniards. The park was once part of the grounds of the nearby **Hotel Santa Catalina**, which is an impressive, luxury hotel that was built by the British in 1890. It attracts many visiting celebrities and royalty. Designed by Néstor de la Torre, its white walls perfectly set off the ornate wooden balconies. The hotel faces a delightful circular plaza complete with an ancient dragon tree. The Hotel Santa Catalina is also the location for the city's **Casino** which is open from Monday to Thursday (20:00–04:00) and on Fridays and Saturdays (20:00–15:00). It offers French and American roulette, blackjack, poker and slot machines.

Also in the Parque Doramas is the **Pueblo Canario**, a sort of model Canary Island village, which was set up in 1939 based on the ideas of the De la Torre brothers. The *pueblo* is unashamedly aimed at tourists and has shops

BY CAR OR COACH?

Most visitors to Gran Canaria stay in the resorts in the south of the island, such as Maspalomas or Playa del Inglés. For them, a day trip to Las Palmas should be an essential part of the holiday. There are three main ways to get there. The majority of tourists make use of organized **coach** trips, although these tend to concentrate on shopping and because of the afternoon closing times, they only spend half the day in the city. Other visitors hire **cars**, but the main problem with this option is being able to find a parking space. The best bet is the underground car park at Parque Santa Catalina, although you need to find other means of transport to the historic quarter of the city from here. A third possibility is to take a **bus** to Las Palmas. These run at half hourly intervals from the south of the island.

Right: *Life in Las Palmas revolves around the Parque de Santa Catalina, a busy tree-lined square with outdoor cafes.*

selling Canarian handicrafts as well as numerous restaurants. A highlight is the performance of traditional singing and dancing, in full national costume, which takes place twice a week (on Thursdays at 17:30 and on Sundays at 11:45) and entrance is free. The small tourist office in the *pueblo* is also open at these times. One of the houses in the pueblo has been turned into the **Museo Néstor**, to celebrate the work of Gran Canaria's most famous artist, Néstor Martín Fernández de la Torre. In addition to his paintings there are stage sets and furniture that he designed on display. It is open from Tuesday to Friday (10:00–13:00 and 16:00–20:00) and on Saturday and Sunday (11:00–14:00) and the admission charge is small. The Parque Doramas also has a small zoo, some sport facilities and a botanical garden. The central part of Las Palmas concludes with the **Cuidad Jardín** (a garden city), which was laid out by the British at the end of the 19th century. It consists largely of villas, many in British colonial style, along tree-lined avenues.

NORTHERN LAS PALMAS

The northern part of the city narrows rapidly into an isthmus joining the 'mainland' with the former island of La Isleta. North of Cuidad Jardín is the busy commercial district of **Alcaravaneras**. The Avenida Mesa y López

---

BENITO PÉREZ GALDÓS (1843–1920)

Galdós is considered to be one of Spain's greatest novelists. He spent the first 19 years of his life in Las Palmas, before moving to Madrid in 1862. He wrote nearly 100 novels and historical books, rich in social commentary. He is often described as the 'Spanish Charles Dickens'. Being a committed socialist, he initially found life difficult in the conservative Spain of the time. One of his most famous works was entitled *Forntunata y Jacinta* and it is the story of two unhappily married women from different social classes. One of Galdós's novels has been filmed and his portrait has appeared on a Spanish banknote. Strangely, none of his works were set in his native Canary Islands.

crosses the district and on the western side is the **Plaza de España**, which has a large number of outdoor cafés. Located on both sides of the *avenida* (wide, tree-lined street) is the fine quality Spanish department store, **El Corte Inglés**. This is a shopper's delight and both branches have very good, top-floor restaurants. The coastal side of the district has a small beach, the **Playa de las Alcaravaneras**, which is a popular spot for beach sports, but rather too near the docks to be recommended for swimming.

Parque de Santa Catalina *

We now reach the heart of the modern city, the **Santa Catalina** district, where life revolves particularly around the **Parque de Santa Catalina**. The name is misleading, since it is less of a park and more of a bustling city square. Shoeshine boys, peddlers and lottery ticket sellers mingle with the tourists, office workers, and seamen from the ships in the port. The tables of numerous restaurants spill out under the palm trees, alongside the ranks for taxis and horse-drawn carriages. The city's main

Northern Las Palmas de Gran Canaria

> ### THE CHANGING FACE OF THE PUERTO DE LA LUZ
>
> Throughout its history the port of Las Palmas has been one of the busiest Spanish ports. It is situated in the centre of the traffic from Europe, Africa and the Americas and this has always been the reason for its pre-eminence. It has traditionally played a major role in providing supplies and fuel for transatlantic vessels, offering a haven for the fishing fleets and navies from many nations and a port of call for cruise liners. All of these essential functions are being challenged today. The melting of the Cold War has lessened its importance as a naval base and cruise liners seem to prefer Santa Cruz on Tenerife or Los Mármoles on Lanzarote, while the Russian fishing fleet has needed financial inducements in order to stay. A major scheme is needed to revitalize the port and prevent further decline.

tourist office is located in a corner of the square. Visitors arriving by car will find that there is a convenient underground car park beneath the *parque*. The streets leading off the square are full of shops and bazaars selling electronic goods, liquor, handicrafts, jewellery, embroidered items and clothing – bargaining with the merchants is strongly encouraged! Ethnic restaurants and the occasional sex shop complete the scene.

Playa de las Canteras **

At this point, the two sides of the narrow isthmus present a great contrast. To the west is the **Playa de las Canteras**, the beach where modern tourism started in Gran Canaria. The fine white sands stretch for 4km (2.5 miles) and can be crowded, particularly on summer weekends. An offshore reef, **La Barra**, protects the beach from the strong Atlantic waves, creating a safe lagoon for swimmers, who are watched by lifeguards. Surfers favour the southern end of the beach, where the waves crash in unhindered. Playa de las Canteras is less frequented by foreign visitors, who prefer the sunnier south of the island, but remains popular with Spaniards. Sun loungers are available for hire, along with pedalos and other craft. Behind the beach is a traffic-free promenade, lined with hotels, apartment blocks and restaurants, as well as nightclubs.

Left: *The 16th-century Castillo de la Luz now houses an arts centre.*
Opposite: *Playa de las Canteras is the city's best beach, but it is more popular with locals than foreign visitors.*

Puerto de la Luz

On the eastern side of the isthmus, in contrast, is the **Puerto de la Luz** – the Harbour of Light. The port of Las Palmas has always provided fuel and supplies for transatlantic shipping and it expanded considerably at the end of the 19th century. Today it claims to be the largest port in Spain and the Las Palmas fishing fleet is the biggest in the country. A number of ferries use the port and it is also popular with transatlantic yachtsmen who use the **Muelle Deportivo** just to the south of the ferry terminal. There are also a few naval vessels to be seen, although Las Palmas has played less of a strategic role since the end of the Cold War, as NATO navies have not needed to refuel at Las Palmas. However, a certain amount of dilapidation has set in and the local authorities are taking a serious look at ways to restore the port. Guarding the northern end of the port is the **Castillo de la Luz**, a fortress that was built in 1493 to defend the town against pirates. It has recently been renovated and it is now the venue for occasional art exhibitions.

For a stunning view over Las Palmas, drive (or take the No. 41 bus) to the top of **La Isleta**. This former island rises to the height of 239m (784ft) and is home to the local fishermen.

REDUNDANT HOTELS

When the tourist boom began in Gran Canaria in the late 1960s, it was the capital, Las Palmas, that emerged as the main holiday resort around the Playa de las Canteras. In subsequent years the focus of the tourist industry moved to the purpose-built resorts in the drier, sunnier south of the island. Although the Playa de las Canteras remains popular with visiting Spaniards from the mainland and with *Canarios* (particularly at weekends), a number of hotels have had to close. At the height of its popularity Las Palmas provided tourists with 30,000 beds, but only 10,000 are required today. The redundant hotels have now been converted to serve other purposes. Some have become residential apartment blocks, including social housing, while others are used as government offices. Some of the older hotels have simply been demolished.

Las Palmas de Gran Canaria at a Glance

BEST TIMES TO VISIT

Although Las Palmas is located in the wetter north of the island, its coastal position means that it misses much of the cloud and rain that is found at higher altitudes. From a climatic point of view, any time of the year is suitable for a visit to the capital, although some find the summer heat rather trying. Two special times of the year are at **Carneval**, which takes place in **February**, and **Corpus Christi** in early **June**.

GETTING THERE

Las Palmas can be reached from the other islands in the Canary archipelago by the **ferries** run by Companía Trasmediterránea and Líneas Fred Olsen. Trasmediterránea also has a ferry route to Las Palmas from Cadíz in mainland Spain. On Gran Canaria itself it is possible to reach Las Palmas from Gando Airport, by **shuttle**, **bus** or **taxi** within half an hour. **Public service buses**, run by the Utinsa, cover the north of the island and include the airport. Tour groups run **coach excursions** from the main resorts to Las Palmas. Visitors who **hire cars** are able to reach the city from the resorts in the south, using the motorway, in under an hour.

GETTING AROUND

A problem for visitors to Las Palmas is that the main areas of interest – **Vegueta** and **Triana, Parque Doramas**

and **Santa Catalina** – are far from one another and covering all three on foot could be extremely tiring. Fortunately **bus** No.1 links all three districts, while **taxis** are cheap and plentiful.

WHERE TO STAY

Accommodation that varies in price and quality is available.

LUXURY
Hotel Santa Catalina, Parque Doramas, tel: 928 243040, fax: 928 242764. A historic building with a casino favoured by royalty and celebrities.
Hotel Imperial Playa, Calle Ferreras 1, tel: 928 468854. Dominating the northern end of Las Canteras beach, with a pool, sauna and squash courts.
Meliá Las Palmas, Calle Gomera 6, tel: 928 267600, fax: 928 268411. A large, modern hotel with a pool and shops overlooking the beach.
Los Bardinos, Calle Eduardo Benot 3, tel: 928 266100, fax: 928 229139. A 23-storey block with a rooftop pool and restaurant.

MID-RANGE
Astoria, Calle Fernando Guanateme 54, tel: 928 222750, fax: 928 272499. Mid-sized hotel with pool and squash courts.
Cantur, Calle Sagasta 28, tel: 928 273000, fax: 928 272373. A friendly atmosphere near the beach.

Madrid, Plazoleta de Cairasco 2, tel: 928 360664. Once a luxury hotel, now neglected. Franco stayed here before starting his coup in 1936.

BUDGET
Pensione Princessa, Calle Princessa Guayarmina 2, tel: 982 467704. Basic rooms only a few blocks from the beach.
Majórica, Calle de Ripoche 22, tel: 928 262878. In a noisy area at Parque de Santa Catalina, but it is clean, neat and cheap.
Tamabada, Calle Pelayo 1, tel: 928 262000. Small, modest hotel in the southern part of Playa Las Canteras.

WHERE TO EAT

Visitors to Las Palmas are spoilt with a wide range of food to choose from. In addition to traditional Canarian and Spanish mainland cooking, there is cuisine from all over the world available at prices to suit all pockets.

LUXURY
Hotel Reina Isabel, Calle Alfredo L. Jones 40, tel: 928 260100. Marvellous grill room on the 8th floor, with views over the Atlantic.
La Casita, Calle León y Castillo 227, tel: 928 234699. An elegant terrace dining-room near Parque Doramas, very popular with the city's middle class .
Julio Marisquería, Calle La Naval 132, Puerto de La Luz,

Las Palmas de Gran Canaria at a Glance

tel: 928 460139. Probably the best seafood in town.

MID-RANGE

Casa Pepe Lucán, Calle Joaquín Costa 25, tel: 928 26373. Traditional Canarian dishes with a cult following of locals.

Meson Condado, Calle de Ferraras 22, tel: 928 224824. Galician and mainland food, particularly fish and shellfish.

Pat's Place, Calle Galileo 5, tel: 928 262563. If a full English breakfast, roast beef and Yorkshire pudding and fish and chips are what you want, then this is the place.

BUDGET

For inexpensive food try the various branches of American fast food chains such as **KFC** and **McDonalds** or alternatively some of the many **pizzerias**. There are many cheap **Chinese** restaurants. A tour round the ***tapas*** bars may end up being more expensive than a set meal. Many restaurants offer a ***menu del día*** (the menu of the day), which usually includes a generous three-course meal for a very reasonable price.

El Cerdo que Ríe (The Laughing Pig), tel: 928 271731, and **El Gallo Felíz** (The Happy Cockerel), tel: 928 271731, are two large, popular restaurants owned by the same chain on the Paseo de Las Canteras.

SHOPPING

Las Palmas is something of a shopper's paradise. It is a duty free port, so goods from all round the world are on sale at bargain prices. The main shopping districts are in **Triana**, the area around Calle Mesa y López where the large department store **El Corte Inglés** is located, and the streets around **Parque de Santa Catalina**. In the latter are a number of **bazaars** run by Indians and bargaining is a must. The best buys are electronic goods, handicraft items, ceramics (particularly the Lladro high-quality, porcelain figurines), perfume and tobacco. Visitors staying in self-catering apartments could visit the city's two markets, the **Mercado de Vegueta** and the **Mercado del Puerto**, for delicious fresh fruit and vegetables.

TOURS AND EXCURSIONS

Despite its position in the extreme northeast of the island, tours can be arranged from Las Palmas to all parts of Gran Canaria. Particularly popular are excursions to the

ancient towns of **Teror** and **Telde**, the volcanic crater at **Pico de Bandama**, the **Dedo de Dios** at Puerto de las Nieves and the **Jardín Botánico Canario** botanical gardens near Tafira.

The most reliable travel agents include **Viajes Insular** at Calle de Luis Morote 9, tel: 928 227950, who are also the representatives of American Express on the island, and **Viajes Halcón** at Calle del General Vives 77, tel: 928 279406.

USEFUL CONTACTS

Tourist information offices: the main one in Las Palmas is in the corner of Parque de Santa Catalina, open Monday to Friday (09:00–14:00). There is another office in the Pueblo Canario, but this is only open when performances take place on Thursdays and Sundays. The *ayuntmiento* (the town hall) in Plaza Santa Ana in Vegueta provides a small amount of information and there is also a small information booth next to the El Corte Inglés store on Avenida Mesa y Lopéz.

LAS PALMAS	J	F	M	A	M	J	J	A	S	O	N	D
AVERAGE TEMP. °F	64	66	66	68	70	72	79	81	81	79	75	72
AVERAGE TEMP. °C	18	19	19	20	21	22	26	27	27	26	24	22
HOURS OF SUN DAILY	7	7	8	8	9	9	10	8	8	8	7	6
RAINFALL in	1.3	1	1	0.7	0.3	0	0	0	2	1	2	1.5
RAINFALL mm	32	24	24	18	8	0	0	0	53	27	52	39
DAYS OF RAINFALL	7	6	5	4	2	0	0	0	2	6	10	9

3
The North

As with most of the other islands in the archipelago, the north of Gran Canaria is the wettest, greenest and – in many ways – the most attractive part of the island. The fertile volcanic soil is watered by the rain brought by the trade winds, allowing a wide variety of subtropical crops to be grown, although many fruits – such as bananas – still require irrigation. The land is extensively cultivated, with terraced slopes stretching far into the hills.

The northern coastal strip is the most densely populated part of the island, with a network of hamlets, villages and towns. Amongst the towns are ancient settlements such as the home of the prolific sculptor José Luján Pérez, **Santa María de Guía**, the ecclesiastic capital of the island, **Teror**, and **Arucas** with its imposing Gaudi-inspired church.

There are numerous remnants of the preconquest Guanches; **Gáldar**, in the west, was one of the ancient Guanche capitals and nearby are the **Cueva Pintada** (Painted Caves) and the **Cenobio de Valerón**, a honeycomb of caves, which are believed to have been used for grain storage.

The northern coastline is generally low-lying, rocky and somewhat uninspiring, but the occasional fishing village, such as **Puerto Sardina**, is well worth a visit for its excellent seafood restaurants. Heading further inland, the roads can be quite tortuous as they wind around the *barrancos*, so be prepared as journeys can take a lot longer than anticipated.

DON'T MISS

*** Teror: Gran Canaria's religious centre, with cobbled streets and squares and fine Canarian architecture.
*** Cenobia de Valerón: these caves near Guía are the island's best-preserved archaeological site.
** The church at Arucas: inspired by Gaudi's La Sagrada Família at Barcelona.
** Reptilandia: various reptiles of the world are on show at this unique theme park near Gáldar.

Opposite: *The old part of the town of Teror is noted for its historic buildings and flower displays.*

CLIMATE

Although the north is the wetter side of the island, it only has a moderate rainfall and this falls mainly in the winter months. Cloud increases inland, particularly above 500m (1641ft). Winter temperatures are agreeable, but in summer – particularly in July and August – temperatures are often over 30°C (86°F), making travelling unpleasant without an air-conditioned car.

Below: *Agricultural terraces line the coastal strip west of Las Palmas.*

THE COAST

A motorway leads westwards out of Las Palmas and travels past factories, shanty houses and littered *barrancos*. Not an inspiring introduction to the area, but the scenery soon improves. The road hugs the rugged coastline and the first interesting place is **Bañaderos**, where hollows in the wave-cut platforms are used as swimming pools and for salt production.

The coastal road then leads to the town of **Santa María de Guía** (usually just known as Guía), which was founded by Genoese merchants. It has some impressive domestic architecture and the main square has a decidedly colonial atmosphere. Dominating the square is the Church of Santa María, which has a neoclassical façade designed by the Canary Islands' best known sculptor, José Luján Pérez, who was a native of the town. The church is in many ways a museum to his memory and the interior exhibits many of his works. The French composer, Camille Saint-Saens (1835–1921), also lived in the town for a number of years. Some of his works are said to be inspired by Canarian folk music. Saint-Saens donated the clock on the right-hand side of the two church towers.

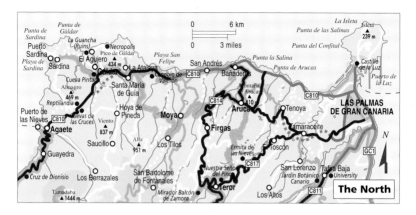

Guía is an important craft centre, producing some fine basketwork. It is also well known for its cheese, called *queso de flor*. It is made from goats' milk and flavoured with artichoke flowers. There are a number of cheese shops in the town, where tasting is encouraged before purchasing.

Just a few kilometres west of Guía is **Gáldar**, situated on the side of the Pico de Gáldar volcano, which rises to 434m (1391ft) and has been accurately described as resembling a slag heap. As with many towns in the north of Gran Canaria, the initial impression is not favourable, but the main square, with its shady laurels and the Church of Santiago de los Caballerosare, is very pleasant. The church, which was built in the 19th century, is thought to have been constructed on the site of a Guanche palace. The interior has a number of works by José Luján Pérez and a font which is believed to have come from Andalucía and used in the baptisms of converted Guanches. Also in the square is the neoclassical *ayuntamiento* (town hall). Have a look inside and see the courtyard, which has an impressive dragon tree, reputed to be over 300 years old. Gáldar was once the capital of Gran Canaria and has many connections with the Guanches. It should really be an important tourist destination, but the town has a rather forlorn air, with high unemployment caused by the decline in banana farming.

JOSÉ LUJÁN PÉREZ (1756–1815)

No important church in the Canary Islands is without the work of Luján Pérez, who was the most significant sculptor produced in the archipelago. He was born, and spent most of his life, in the town of Santa María de Guía in the north of Gran Canaria. The church in Guía is like a museum to his memory, with numerous statues and other memorobilia. José Luján Pérez's work was mainly religious. He carved in wood and the statues were later gilded. His style lived on in the work of his pupil Fernando Estévez (1788–1854), a native of La Orotava in Tenerife.

Above: *Part of the Cueva Pintada (the Painted Cave) at Gáldar.*
Opposite: *One of more than 300 caves in the Cenobio de Valerón complex near Guía.*

GUANCHE CONNECTIONS

Gáldar was the seat of one of two Guanche kingdoms that were in existence before the Spanish Conquest (the other was at Telde in the east). Some public sculptures in the town commemorate this heritage, such as the one of three Guanche princesses and another of the last of the Guanche chiefs, Tenesor Semidan, who persuaded his people to surrender and accept the Spanish as well as their religion.

Cenobio de Valerón ★★★

There are also a number of **archaeological sites** in the area; just southeast of Guía is the remarkable **Cenobio de Valerón**, a series of more than 300 caves behind a massive rock arch. Some of the caves are natural, but the majority have been carved by man, as the volcanic rock, tufa, is soft. Many caves are linked to tunnels and steps. The word *cenobio* means convent and for many years it was thought that the cave complex was the home of *harimaguadas*, noblewomen of Guanche times, who were fattened up and prepared for motherhood here, but recent evidence suggests that the caves were no more than a granary store. The caves indicate a high degree of social organisation and considerable construction skills, especially if you consider that the Guanches had no knowledge of metals and must have dug the caves with bones and sharp stones. The caves are approached through the archway by a series of narrow steps, but entrance into the caves is not allowed, due to sporadic rock falls. Nevertheless, the caves can be appreciated from the outside and it is worthwhile remembering that this is the only archaeological site on Gran Canaria that is open to the public. The Cenobio de Valerón can be viewed Wednesday to Sunday (10:00–17:00), but be prepared for irregular opening hours. On the cliff top above the caves is a *tagoror* (a Guanche meeting place), although there is little to see apart from a few eroded stone benches placed in a rough circle.

Cueva Pintada

The centre of Gáldar is the location of undoubtedly the most important Guanche site in the whole of the Canary Islands. This is the **Cueva Pintada** (the Painted Cave) which was discovered in 1873. Ceramic artefacts and a number of human skeletons were found in the cave, and

THE TROGLODYTE TENDENCY

To suggest that some of the inhabitants of Gran Canaria still lived in caves would surprise any visitor to the island. This statement is, in fact, true, but the situation is not as simple as it first seems. There is a long history of cave dwelling in Gran Canaria, stretching as far back as the time of the Guanches. Today there are a number of families living in 'cave houses' in various parts of the island, including the fishing village of Playa de Sardina in the north. From the outside they look like normal houses, but closer inspection shows that behind the windows and doors, the rest of the house extends back into the rocky hillside. Inside, there may be several cave rooms and some of the homes have small chimneys, allowing the smoke to escape from the fires and kitchen. Many people are reluctant to leave their cave homes, as they have all the modern conveniences of 21st-century living and when the homes need another room, they simply cut it out of the soft volcanic ash. Furthermore, the temperature within the caves remains constant throughout the year.

it is thought that burials might have taken place here. The most remarkable discovery was the cave's walls that were decorated with geometric patterns in the form of circles, squares and triangles. The cave has not been open to the public for some time, as the humid climate damages the paintings. Archaeological work continues and the cave may reopen some time in the future. In the meantime visitors will have to make do with an accurate mock-up of the cave in the Museo Canario in Las Palmas.

Necropolis

Gáldar's other archaeological site is a **necropolis** (known as **Tumuló de la Guancha**), some 2km (1.2 miles) out of town near the coastal village of **El Agujero**. Surrounded by banana plantations are ruins of what is thought to have been mausoleums. Some mummies, dating from the 11th century, were discovered here in the 1930s along with a few items, which might have been used in burials. Theories suggest that the site might have been royal apartments and rooms for *harimaguadas* (*see* page 58). Lack of funds has prevented further archaeological studies and the area is now fenced off and can only be viewed from a distance.

Opposite: *The numerous colourful fishing boats at Playa de Sardina.*
Right: *The Museo Canario has many examples of Guanche pottery, which was made by the coil method, rather than using the wheel.*

Playa de Sardina *

A place that's well worth visiting along this part of the coast is the little fishing village of **Playa de Sardina**, which is tucked between the cliffs and the sea. Close inspection will show that many of the village houses are in fact cave dwellings, with a façade built to make them look like normal houses. The local fishing fleet ensures that all the harbour-side restaurants serve outstanding seafood at very reasonable prices. Enjoy Playa de Sardina while you can, because it seems to be ripe for development.

INLAND

The inland route back to Las Palmas is much slower and more tortuous than the coastal motorway, as the narrow roads negotiate steep-sided *barrancos* and wind between both the plantations and the farms.

Reptilandia **

A diversion to the south of Sardina leads to **Reptilandia**, a theme park with over a thousand snakes, crocodiles, turtles and chameleons. Other attractions include monkeys and poisonous toads. The star exhibits are the Komodo dragons (the world's largest lizards) from Indonesia, and the younger visitors thoroughly enjoy watching the crocodiles being fed. Reptilandia is open daily from 11:00 to 17:30. Nearby this theme park is the village of **Hoya de Pineda**, where women still make pottery in the traditional Guanche style.

TOMÁS MORALES (1885–1921)

Tomás Morales qualified as a doctor in Madrid and became the islands' best known modernist poet in his tragically short life. His most famous work is his anthology, *Las Rosas de Hercules*, but he also wrote plays and newspaper articles. His birthplace, in Moya, is now a museum and it contains many first editions of his poems, some of which are enlarged on the walls. Morales died in Agaete at the early age of 37.

Above: *A specimen from Reptilandia theme park, located north of Agaete.*
Opposite: *Crates of Firgas bottled water. This natural spring water is enjoyed throughout the island.*

Moya *

The road leads inland towards **Moya**, where the most impressive sight is the village church, the **Iglesia el Pilar**, positioned right on the edge of the local *barranco*. It is no surprise to learn that a previous church slipped over the precipitous cliff edge, due to erosive undercutting. The only other interesting feature in Moya is the **Casa Museo Tomás Morales**, which is located in the main square. It was the home of the modernist poet Tomás Morales (1884–1921), who gave up a career in medicine to concentrate on his writing (*see* page 61). At the far end of Barranco de Moya is the area known as **Los Tilos**, one of the last surviving tracts of laurel forest that once covered Gran Canaria (it is now clear that it was the felling of the laurel trees that was a major factor in the rainfall reduction on the island). Moya was also reputedly the childhood home of **Doramas** the last Guanche *guanarteme* (king), who died resisting the Spanish invaders. A mountain peak outside the town is named after him (*see* page 67).

Firgas

To the east of Moya is the town of **Firgas**, famous throughout the Canary Islands for its natural spring water. The springs are just to the south of the town and the plant claims to bottle over 250,000 litres a day. This company has put much back into the community, building a stepped *paseo* (promenade) lined with tiled seats and coats of arms of neighbouring towns. Further south is the **Mirador Balcón de Zamora**, one of the best *miradors* (viewpoints) on the island. From the restaurant's terrace there are fine views over the town of Teror and across to Las Palmas.

Teror ***

The inland route now reaches **Teror** which, despite its name, is a peaceful place with a population of around 10,000. Teror is full of traditional Canarian architecture and few would disagree with the claim that it is the most attractive town on the island. The imposing, stone town houses have richly carved wooden balconies and window frames. Head for the central **Plaza de Nuestra Señora del Pino** and the neighbouring **Calle Real** to see vernacular architecture at its best. Dominating the

CÉSAR MANRIQUE

The artist, sculptor and environmentalist, César Manrique, has had an enormous influence on the landscape of the Canary Islands. He was born in Lanzarote in 1920 and established a reputation as a painter, working on mainland Spain and in North America. He returned to Lanzarote in 1968 and thereafter devoted much of his time saving the Canary Islands from the worst consequences of mass tourism, particularly in the field of architecture. His essential approach was that buildings should be in harmony with the natural landscape around them. His best work can be seen in Lanzarote, but he also had a considerable influence over recent architectural developments in Gran Canaria. Sadly, Manrique died in a car accident in 1992.

Opposite: *Traditional old houses have survived in the beautiful town of Teror.*
Below: *The basilica at Teror, the home of the image of La Virgen del Pino, Gran Canaria's patron saint.*

square is the **Basilica de la Virgen del Pino**, which contains the figure of the Virgen del Pino, Gran Canaria's patron saint. The present basilica dates from the end of the 18th century, when it replaced a former building that was destroyed by an explosion in 1718. Pilgrims flock to the basilica throughout the year, but particularly on the island's most important fiesta, the day of Virgen del Pino, held in early September. The interior of the basilica is full of interest. It has three aisles supported by dark basalt columns with attractive, honey-coloured capitals. The church is rich with paintings and contains a number of statues by José Luján Pérez. Also in the shady central square is a 17th-century house known as the **Casa Museo Patrones de la Virgen del Pino**. This is

the residence of the Manrique de Lara family who have been custodians of the Virgen del Pino figure for several centuries. The house is open as a museum when the family is not at home and contains some fine paintings, porcelain and furniture. It is possible to roam around the bedrooms and the kitchen, while the stables are also fascinating and display, amongst other things, a Triumph car and the state coach of Alfonso XII. Other interesting buildings in the square include the **Town Hall** and the **Bishop's Palace**, part of which is now a cultural centre. Leading off the Plaza del Pino is a smaller square, the **Plaza Teresa de Bolívar**, which was named after the wife of Simon Bolívar, the founder of Bolivia. She was born in Teror and her family's coat of arms can be seen in the square along with a bust of her husband. Take some time to wander around the traffic-free centre of Teror and appreciate its cobbled alleyways, hidden squares and fine domestic architecture.

Arucas **

The final ancient settlement in the north of Gran Canaria is **Arucas**, the third largest town on the island with a population of 27,000. Its huge church, the **Iglesia de San Juan Bautista**, dominates Arucas. Built of dark blue-grey basalt, it has towering spires and pinnacles and some commendable modern stained glass. The main

Above: *The Iglesia de San Juan Bautista towers like a cathedral over the town of Arucas.*

Opposite: *An information board illustrates the story of rum making in the Arucas area.*

tower is 60m (197ft) high, the tallest in the Canary Islands. The church is said to have been inspired by Antonio Gaudi's La Sagrada Família Cathedral in Barcelona and visitors can easily see the resemblance. The construction of the church began in 1909 and it was only completed in 1977. There are some interesting art works inside the church, including the impressive *Reclining Christ* by Manuel Ramos. The Gourié family, who own the local rum factory, sponsored the church. They also donated their town house as a **museum** and its gardens are now the **municipal park**, outside of which is an attractive fountain.

Those wishing to see the **rum factory** may find the visit a little crowded since organized tour groups often frequent the works. The factory is located just to the north of the town on the C814. The rum (or *ron* as it is known is Gran Canaria) is made under the brand name of *Arehucas* and some 3.5 million litres (6.2 million pints) are produced each year. The factory also produces *ron miel*, a rum and honey liqueur. Alongside the factory is a small **museum**, illustrating the history of rum making in the Arucas area. The rum is made from sugar cane, which was once a thriving industry in the district.

Nowadays, not enough is produced locally and the shortfall is imported from abroad. Visitors to the factory can sample the products and also see rum barrels that have been autographed by visiting celebrities and royalty. The factory and museum are open from Monday to Friday (10:00–14:00).

Just to the north of Arucas is the **Montaña de Arucas**, believed to be the place where the Guanche leader, Doramas, died in 1481. This old volcanic cone rises to 410m (1345ft) and its *mirador* (with restaurant) provides views of the entire northern coast of the island, from Las Palmas in the east to Sardina in the west.

THE RISE AND FALL OF SUGAR PRODUCTION

The history of the Canary Islands is filled with economic boom and bust cycles. One of the first examples of this came about with the growing of sugar cane. The crop was introduced by the Portuguese from Madeira and financed by Genoese merchants. The first sugar mill was built at Agaete in the year after the conquest was completed (1484). The work in the fields was done by share-croppers from Madeira, but the heavy work in the refineries was carried out by black slaves. The boom in the sugar trade was not to last. The countries of the New World soon established their own sugar industries and their more appropriate climatic conditions enabled them to undercut the produce of the Canary Islands. A further blow came with the abolition of the slave trade. Nowadays, a small amount of sugar is grown in the north of the island around Arucas, but this is not even enough to supply the local rum-making industry and extra supplies have to be imported.

The North at a Glance

BEST TIMES TO VISIT

The northern part of Gran Canaria is a pleasant place to visit at any time of the year, although there is a greater possibility of rain and cloud during the winter months (**November** to **February**). Conversely, the heat can be extremely trying during the summer months, especially in **July** and **August**.

GETTING THERE

The area can easily be reached by **car** from the southern resorts and by taking the motorway from Las Palmas. Alternatively, UTINSA **buses** operate services from Las Palmas, and the car **ferry** from Tenerife docks at Puerto de las Nieves in the west.

GETTING AROUND

As regular **bus** services between the towns in the north of Gran Canaria are few and far between, the only viable way of travelling around the area is by **hired car**, and some cars can be prebooked on the internet from anywhere in the world with companies such as Holiday Autos, website: www.holidayautos.co.uk The coastal route is the best option. It is quick and convenient, but the inland roads are usually indirect and slow, which means that most journeys will probably take longer than expected.

Remember to take a good road map with you as some of the rural routes are badly signposted. **Coach** tours only visit the more popular places in this region.

WHERE TO STAY

Accommodation can be something of a problem in the northern part of Gran Canaria, since the area is so easily accessible from Las Palmas and the south of the island that very few people, even businessmen, need to stay in the region. The lack of coastal resorts is also a factor, and there is certainly no accommodation in the luxury range.

MID-RANGE
Hotel Princesa Guayarmina, Via Los Berrazales, 8km (5 miles) to the east of Agaete, tel: 928 898009, fax: 928 898525. This is an old spa hotel with thermal pool.
Hotel Hacienda de Anzo, Gáldar, tel/fax: 928 551655. A simple country house which has been converted into a delightful hotel. It has its own swimming pool and a lovely garden.

BUDGET
El Cortijo, Camino de Hoyes del Cavadero 11, Ctra de Moya a Fontanales km 21, Fontanales, tel: 928 610285. A small, rural hotel, perfect for hikers.

Hotel Bella, Calle Panchito Hemandez 10, Arucas, tel: 928 600651. This is a most conveniently situated little urban hotel.
Youth Hostel, on the outskirts of Santa María de Guía, tel: 928 882728. This is Gran Canaria's only youth hostel, although it would generally be a last resort for most of the area's visitors .

WHERE TO EAT

There is very little in the luxury range in the rural areas of the north, and the restaurants in the area generally serve simple country Canarian food. The better places are crowded with people from Las Palmas over weekends. Of particular interest are the wonderful seafood restaurants in the coastal villages such as Sardina.

MID-RANGE
El Secuestro, Plaza de Nuestra Señora del Pino, Teror. This is a very popular rustic centre-of-town restaurant noted particularly for its meat dishes. It is usually crowded over weekends with visitors from Las Palmas.
Mesón Los Parranderos, Calle de la Diputación 6, Teror (near the main square). This centrally located restaurant has a reasonably priced set menu, ideal for those visitors wandering around the old town.

The North at a Glance

Restaurant Meson de la Montana de Arucas, Montana de Fuego s/n, tel: 928 601475. This restaurant offers not only good food, but also fabulous views from the terrace.

Casa Placido, Calle Simón Milián 5, Moya. This eatery serves very good local dishes, including a cheap *menu del día*, at tables overlooking the beautiful *barranco* at Moya. No telephone.

Restaurante Alcori, Calle Capitán Quesada, Gáldar, tel: 928 882712. Very generous portions of good food are served at this popular, busy and centrally located restaurant.

Bar Restaurante Balcón de Zamora, just to the south of Teror; Ctra. De Vega de San Mateo, tel: 928 618042. Simple Canarian food is served at this restaurant, with a beautiful view.

For **seafood** restaurants, head for the fishing port of **Sardina**. The following are recommended: **Fragata** (probably the most expensive), tel: 928 883296; **Vistamar** (possibly the cheapest); **Cueva** (as its name suggests, this is a cave restaurant) and **Miguelín** (offering very good value).

BUDGET

A few of the northern towns have Chinese or Indian restaurants as well as American fast-food outlets, but if you would like to try traditional Canarian food, you will have to look around for *tapas* bars in the town centres.

Mesón Casa Plácido, Calle de Alejandro Hidalgo 6, Moya. Cheap and filling menu of the day.

TOURS AND EXCURSIONS

There are a number of tours organized by travel agents, both in Las Palmas and in the resorts in the south of the island. The most popular venue is the **Reptilandia** theme park near Gáldar, which claims to have the largest outdoor collection of reptiles in the world, and is worth a visit. Other tours of the region take in **Arucas**, with its beautiful church and an interesting rum factory. A number of tour companies combine a tour of northern Gran Canaria with a morning's shopping in Las Palmas, and some excursions include **Teror** in their itinerary. Here you can visit the church to see the Virgen del Piño, the island's patron saint. Another popular tour visits **Agaete** and **Puerto de las Nieves** via the banana route. Other tours visit the popular Sunday market at Teror, where various items such as handicrafts, herbs and cheeses can be bought. For tours in the north of the island contact Mathern, tel: 900 713160 (toll free) or tel: 928 732129. Coaches will pick up visitors from a variety of locations in the southern resorts, including all the major hotels. An excellent excursion for keen bird watchers is to the north-western tip of the island, known as the Punta de la Sardina. The lighthouse here is a marvellous position for watching seabirds, including the shearwaters.

SHOPPING

Most of the towns in the north of Gran Canaria have lively outdoor markets, where a variety of local handicrafts can be bought. Different towns have their different specialities: Teror is well known for its baskets, Guía for its bone-handled knives and Arucas for its pottery. Other handicraft items include silk and castanets.

USEFUL CONTACTS

It is important to know that none of the northern towns have an active **tourist information office**, although sometimes the Town Hall provides information, as in the case of the *ayuntmiento* at Arucas, which produces an information brochure. **The Red Cross** is represented in most of the larger towns, such as the following: Arucas, tel: 928 600095; Gáldar, tel: 928 552004; Guía, tel: 928 882222; Moya, tel: 928 610222 and Teror, tel: 928 630190.

4
The Arid East

Due to the climate and physical layout of the island, the eastern side of Gran Canaria is similar to its larger neighbour, Tenerife. The northern part receives an adequate rainfall from the northeast trade winds, but further south the weather is drier and the landscape appears more arid. There are few settlements on the coast, since people were previously driven inland – where the weather is conveniently kinder to agriculture – by buccaneers and pirates. As a result there is a string of market towns, some 10–12km (6–7 miles) inland, such as **Telde**, **Agüimes** and **Ingenio**.

In the north, just southwest of Las Palmas, there is a commuter region, centred on the towns of **Tafira Alta**, **Tafira Baja** and **Santa Brígida**. Here, neoclassical villas stand cheek by jowl only interrupted by tree-lined avenues, smart restaurants and a golf club. To the east is the **Caldera de Bandama**, an extinct volcanic crater over 200m (656ft) deep. To the west lies the **Jardín Botánico Canario**, an area of shady gardens concentrating on the flora of the Canary Islands.

The coastal strip is generally an uninspiring sight for incoming tourists arriving at Gando airport. However, the arid landscape, the *plasticultura* (growing fruit and vegetables under plastic) farming and the stark industrial estates are, fortunately, not a true impression of the island as a whole.

Evidence of the **Guanche** way of life abounds in the region, although few archaeological sites are in a good state of preservation. **Telde**, the ancient capital of the

DON'T MISS

*** Barranco de Guayadeque: observe fine scenery and folklore.
** Jardín Botánico Canario: these gardens provide the finest opportunity to see the island's native plants.
** Caldera de Bandama: view the coast from the peak of this extinct volcanic crater.
* Iglesia San Juan Bautista in Telde: see the most valuable art on the island.
* Parque de Cocodrilos: theme park with crocodiles, alligators, scorpions, snakes and other animals.

Opposite: *Specimen trees in the Jardín Botánico Canario, near Tafira.*

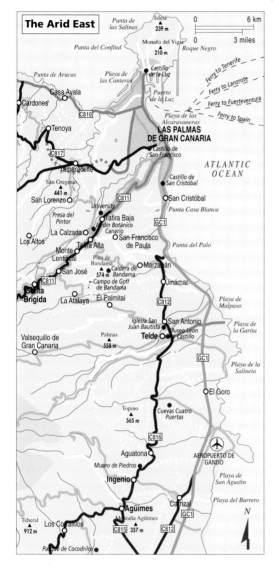

The Arid East

Punta de las Salinas

Isleta ▲ 239 m

0   6 km
0   3 miles

Punta del Confital

Monaña del Vigía ▲ 210 m   Roque Negro

Punta de Arucas   Playa de las Canteras   Castillo de la Luz

Casa Ayala

Cardones

Tenoya

C810

Puerto de la Luz

Ferry to Tenerife
Ferry to Lanzrote
Ferry to Fuerteventura
Ferry to Spain

Playa de las Alcaravaneras

LAS PALMAS DE GRAN CANARIA

C817

Tamaraceite

San Gregorio ▲ 441 m

San Lorenzo

University

Castillo de San Francisco

Castillo de San Cristóbal

ATLANTIC OCEAN

San Cristóbal

Punta Casa Blanca

Presa del Pintor

La Calzada

Los Altos

Tafira Baja

Jardín Botánico Canario

C811

GC1

San Francisco de Paula

Punta del Palo

Monte Lentiscal

Tafira Alta

Pico de Bandama ▲ 574 m

Caldera de Bandama

Marzagán

San José

C811

Campo de Golf de Bandama

Jinámar

Santa Brígida

La Atalaya

El Palmital

C812

Playa de Malpaso

Valsequillo de Gran Canaria

Palmas ▲ 558 m

Iglesia San Juan Bautista

San Antonio

Telde

Museo León y Castillo

Playa de la Garita

GC1

Playa de la Salineta

El Goro

Topino ▲ 565 m

Cuevas Cuatro Puertas

C816

Aguatona

AEROPUERTO DE GANDO

Museo de Piedros

Ingenio

Playa de San Agustín

Playa del Burrero

Teheral ▲ 912 m

Los Corralillos

Agüimes

Carrizal

GC1

Montaña Agüimes ▲ 357 m

N

C815

C812

Parque de Cocodrilos

eastern side of the island, and the **Cuatro Puertas** close by, are worth a visit. There are also numerous caves in the **Barranco de Guayadeque**, in-between **Ingenio** and **Agüimes**. The *barranco* is a popular spot for excursions and tourists flock to the folklore performances that are staged in the valley.

COMMUTER COUNTRY

In Las Palmas the broad dual carriageway that separates Vegueta from Triana leads out of town, via some hairpin bends, to the first of three commuter settlements, **Tafira Baja**. This is also the location where the **University of Gran Canaria**, established in 1989, is situated.

Jardín Botánico Canario **

A turn to the right at the entrance to Tafira Baja takes you to the **Jardín Botánico Canario**. These botanical gardens were opened in 1952 and the aim is to show visitors the endemic plants and trees of the Canary Islands, and instil the responsibility of preservation and replanting. The gardens run along the floor of the **Guiniguada Barranco** and spread up the valley walls. Paths and steps, some of which are quite steep, connect all the different areas. Canarian laurel, which once covered large areas of the islands, as well as numerous tall Canary pines are found here. There is also a sizable cactus garden and a section containing plants from Central and South America. The paths lead up to a lookout point where there is a bust of Don José de Viera y Clavijo, the well-known Canarian naturalist. The gardens have a good restaurant located near the upper entrance, and from here there are excellent views of the lava stream which once flowed down the valley from nearby Monte Lentiscal (this mountain was the spot where the Dutch pirate, Pieter van der Does, was defeated). There is also a Visitors' Centre at the lower end of the gardens, which is open daily (09:00–18:00) and the entrance to this centre is free.

Close to the Jardín Botánico Canario is the hamlet of **La Calzada** and in a nearby gorge there are a series of caves known as the **Cuevas de los Frailes**. It was here where the Guanches murdered the preconquest Spanish monks, known as *frailes*. The C811 route leads up to **Tafira Alta** and on the side of the road is the **Hotel Los**

CLIMATE

The northern and more mountainous parts of the central region attract cloud and some light rain from the northeastern trade winds. The coastal strip becomes progressively arid and windy towards the south. The inland areas can be cool in winter, but summers are less cloudy. The lowland along the coast can be very hot in the summer months, especially when easterly winds drift across from the Sahara.

Below: *A terrapin inhabits one of the pools at the Járdin Botánico Canario.*

THE UNIVERSITY OF GRAN CANARIA

For many years there was only one university in the Canary Islands, at La Laguna in Tenerife. Despite expanding, it could not accommodate the high demand and many *Canarios* were obliged to head to the mainland for their university education. Inter-island rivalry between Gran Canaria and Tenerife led to calls for Gran Canaria to have its own university. It was eventually founded at Tafira Alta, just outside Las Palmas, in 1989. However, it has struggled to gain a reputation and many young people from Gran Canaria prefer to go to mainland Spain to complete their education.

THE BIRD OF PARADISE FLOWER

Gran Canaria has a wide variety of exotic flowers and shrubs that have been introduced to the island from many parts of the world. The favourite of most visitors is the **bird of paradise flower** (*Strelitzia reginae*). They have glossy dark green leaves, flower heads of orange, purple and blue petals, and resemble a crane's head in shape. The flowers make an ideal bedding plant in the parks and hotel gardens of Gran Canaria. If you fancy taking a Strelitzia home, don't bother to take a cutting, because you can buy them at the airport shops, potted and packed for the journey.

Frailes, which was built by the British in the 1890s. Forty years later its guests included Franco and his henchmen who are said to have conspired here just prior to the Spanish Civil War. The road continues to the small market town of **Santa Brígida**. British merchants and businessmen favoured the two Tafiras and Santa Brígida, at the turn of the last century, as they preferred to live here in the clean, cool air rather than in the heat of Las Palmas. As well as luxurious villas, they built a cinema, a golf club and hotels. Today the area is still the most prestigious on the island and it is well known for its excellent restaurants.

Caldera de Bandama **

From Tafira Alta, a road leads east through vineyards and climbs, cutting through banks of black volcanic ash, to the **Pico de Bandama**. This peak rises to 574m (1883ft) and it has a small lookout point and café. The views are stupendous, stretching from Las Palmas in the north to

Gando airport in the south and inland over the Tafiras. From the peak you can look down into the **Caldera de Bandama**. A caldera is a large volcanic crater and this peak is the highest point on the crater rim. The caldera is over 200m (656ft) deep and 1km (0.6 miles) wide. There is a small farm at the bottom of the caldera and it is possible to walk down to it by taking a narrow path alongside the nearby church. There is a golf course, built by the British and said to be the oldest in Spain, in the opposite direction.

Above: *The original* Idolo de Tara, *a Guanche statuette in the Museo Canario in Las Palmas.* **Opposite:** *A view into the vast crater of the Caldera de Bandama, an extinct volcano.*

TELDE

With a population well over 80,000, Telde is the second largest town in Gran Canaria. Before the Spanish Conquest, it was the Guanche capital of the eastern half of the island (the western capital was Gáldar) and it is believed that the heroic Guanche leader, Doramas, lived here. Certainly there must have been a sizable settlement in the area, as some records from the early years of the conquest state that there were over 14,000 Guanche dwellings in either caves or simple houses. It was in one of these settlements, Tara, that the statue known as the *Idolo de Tara* was discovered. The idol has a tiny head and thick short limbs and reproductions of it can be bought all over the island. The original can be seen in the Museo Canario in Las Palmas.

Today Telde has large industrial estates, some dreary-looking suburbs and severe traffic problems, which could deter the visitor. But, as with many towns on the island, it is necessary to head for the historic quarter where there are two old districts, known as **San Juan** and **San Francisco** after their parish churches.

Iglesia San Juan Bautista *

The beautiful **Iglesia San Juan Bautista**, which dates back to 1519, is a particularly striking building, with two grey basalt towers on either side of a white arch with a *Mudéjar* doorway, making a pleasing façade. Dominating the interior is a huge, golden Flemish *retablo*, which diplays six Nativity scenes (this altarpiece is regarded as Gran Canaria's most valuable work of art and for this reason the church is usually closed – the best time to gain access is just before or after a service). There are also statues by José Luján Pérez and his pupil, Fernando Estévez. The most extraordinary statue is a crucifixion, which comes from Mexico. It stands at 2m (6.6ft) and weighs only 8kg (18 pounds) – explained by the fact that it is made of corn cobs! The statue's face, apparently, changes colour with the seasons, but nobody has produced a scientific explanation for this phenomenon. There is an attractive plaza in front of the church surrounded by elegant Canarian town houses, cobbled streets and alleyways. The other attractive part of the town is the *barrio* (district) of **San Francisco**, with old merchants' houses centred around an 18th-century church.

Telde Attractions *

Another interesting building in Telde is the town hall, the **Casa del Conde de la Vega**, once the home of the count who was responsible for the development of the tourist resorts in the south of the island. The only museum in the town is the **Museo León y Castillo**, once the

---

GOLF ON GRAN CANARIA

While neighbouring Tenerife has no fewer than eight golf courses, Gran Canaria has only two. One of these, however, has the reputation of being the oldest golf club in Spain. This is the Club de Golf Bandama, which was founded by the British in 1891. Although it is only a nine-hole course, it is very popular with Japanese visitors. Most tourists looking for a game of golf would be better advised to try the Campo de Golf de Bandama close to the dunes at Maspalomas. As golf is a very popular sport in Spain, it is no surprise to learn that two more courses are planned in Gran Canaria.

home of Juan León y Castillo who built the harbour at Las Palmas. The museum contains articles and exhibits belonging to both Juan and his more famous brother Fernando who became Foreign Minister of Spain. Entrance to the museum, at Calle León y Castillo 43, is free and it is open Monday (17:00–19:00), Tuesday and Friday (10:00–13:00) and Saturday (10:00–13:00).

There are a number of archaeological sites on the outskirts of Telde, but most of them have been neglected over the years and are not worth visiting. An exception is the **Montaña de las Cuatro Puertas** (the Hill of the Four Gates or Doors). The hill, which is close to the C816 on the way to Ingenio, rises to 319m (1047ft) and was once a sacred Guanche site. It consists of a large chamber with four entrances and the marks on the stonework suggest that it was a place of sacrifice. The area in front of the chamber is believed to have been a *tagoror* (an outdoor location where the Guanches held their assemblies – usually under a dragon tree).

INGENIO

Just 8km (5 miles) along the C816 from Telde is the small market town of **Ingenio**. The name means sugar mill in South American Spanish and it was a busy centre of sugar production in the 16th century. There is an interesting **sugar-press monument** on a roundabout near the eastern entrance to the town and, today, other crops such as tomatoes and potatoes are grown in the area. In the attractive square, in the centre of the town, there is a large statue of the *Idolo de Tara* (a copy of a Guanche idol) and the imposing **Church of Our Lady of Candelaria** (the patron saint of the Canary Islands). The Church, with its distinctive towers and white dome, is a local landmark. Another place

---

THE USEFUL CANARY PALM

Common in Gran Canaria, the **Canary Palm** (*Phoenix canariensis*) is grown as an ornamental tree in many parks and gardens. The leaves are an essential raw material for the handicraft industry and they are also used to make mats and baskets. The timber is utilized for construction purposes and the sap is extracted to make palm honey.

Opposite: *The towers of Telde's 16th-century Iglesia San Juan Bautista.*
Below: *The sugar-press monument on a traffic island, Ingenio.*

of interest in Ingenio is the **Museo de Piedras y Artesanía** (the Museum of Rocks and Handicrafts) in the suburb of Mejías. The rocks are of limited interest, but the rest of the museum is an interesting display of Canarian arts and crafts. There is an embroidery school that is attached to the museum and you can watch the craftswomen at work and buy their products. Take a look in the garden, where there are farming implements to be viewed. The museum is open from Monday to Friday (08:00–18:00). Just a couple of kilometres from Ingenio is the old town of **Agüimes**. This was the seat of the Bishops of Gran Canaria between 1483 and 1811 and its church (formerly a cathedral) is impressive. This neoclassical-style church has three aisles and a number of statues by Luján Pérez.

AGÜIMES
Parque de Cocodrilos *

The area around Agüimes is attractive, with cultivated terraced hill slopes providing fruit and vegetables to the resorts in the south. Just outside Agüimes is the theme park, **Parque de Cocodrilos**, which is home to creatures such as crocodiles, alligators, scorpions and snakes. It is open daily (10:00–18:00).

The Barranco de Guayadeque ***

One of the most impressive scenic locations on Gran Canaria is the **Barranco de Guayadeque**, which is a canyon-like valley running inland from Agüimes. The valley floor is flat and water is never very far from the surface, so it is green and lush throughout the year.

THE TALENTED LEÓN Y CASTILLO FAMILY

Almost every town in the Canary Islands has a street or plaza named León y Castillo. It is the name of two brothers who contributed much to the islands. Fernando was a diplomat and politician who rose to the position of Foreign Minister of Spain and was able to obtain dispensation for the development of the Puerto de la Luz at Las Palmas. His brother, Juan, was an engineer who designed and built the port. Their childhood home in Telde is now a museum.

Some of the rarest plants on the island can be found here, including over 80 endemic species, and the whole valley is now classified as a nature reserve. Above the valley floor and cultivation terraces on the lower slopes are steep red cliffs of volcanic ash and other material. The *barranco* had one of the largest Guanche populations on the island and their caves can be seen along the valley side. Huge quantities of archaeological artefacts have been recovered from the caves and these can be seen in the Museo Canario in Las Palmas. Some communities still live in the caves and farm the floor of the valley. You can see cave bars, cave restaurants, cave stores and even a cave church. It is possible to drive for some distance up the valley along a metalled road, but this eventually degenerates into a gravel track. At the the end of the valley there is a famous cave restaurant called the *Tagoror*. The Barranco de Guayadeque is popular with tour groups and coach

Above: *The Barranco de Guayadeque is home to over 80 endemic species of plants.*

Opposite: *Houses in Agüimes showing the traditional pattern of whitewash and dark volcanic stone.*

Below Left: *An unusual sight, a cave bar in the Barranco de Guayadeque.*

Above: *With no fossil fuels or hydro-electric power, Gran Canaria is increasingly turning to wind power in order to generate electricity.*

PLASTICULTURA

Large areas in the southeast of Gran Canaria are covered with plastic greenhouses, under which fruit, vegetables and flowers are grown. The crops are fed through irrigation water pipes, which can be seen over the hillsides bringing water from the reservoirs in the wetter mountainous interior of the island. *Plasticultura* is profitable for the farmer, but it does have its disadvantages. A large amount of water, which is needed by the tourist industry, is used and pesticide residues can build up under the plastic, leaving high levels of chemicals in the crops.

---

trips can be arranged from the resorts in the south. Part of the tour involves watching traditional folk singing and dancing in the caves. The weekends can be over-crowded, as the area is very popular with the local people.

THE ARID COASTAL STRIP

The narrow stretch of land between the mountains and the coast has always been sparsely populated and even fishing villages are few and far between. The dry climate, particularly in the south, has regulated the farming activity in the region. Since the east coast was always subject to raids by pirates – from North Africa and the seafaring nations to the north – the towns are now situated inland.

The tourist who arrives at the airport, and travels either to Las Palmas in the north or to the resorts in the south, will have a bleak impression of the island. The semidesert landscape is covered with billboards, acres of plastic greenhouses producing bananas and tomatoes, the occasional wind farm (where modern windmills generate electricity) and soulless industrial estates. This is hardly the subtropical island of the holiday brochures. There have been some half-hearted attempts at tourist development, notably in the La Garita area close to Telde, but the area suffers from an unattractive environment, strong winds and noise from Gando airport. It is clear that the area will never become a holiday destination to rival the south of the island.

The Arid East at a Glance

BEST TIMES TO VISIT

The higher parts of the east have a **cloud** cover caused by the trade winds. This cloud cover can last for days on end, particularly in the winter months. Pick cloud-free days, if possible, to tour the inland areas. The coastal strip is generally dry and sunny, but it can get unbearably hot over **July** and **August**.

GETTING THERE

The east coast is the most accessible part of the island, as it is convenient to reach from both Gando Airport and Las Palmas.

GETTING AROUND

Hired **cars** are cheaper on Gran Canaria than almost any other part of Europe and a car allows maximum freedom and independence when touring in the region. The green coloured Salcai **buses** serve the north of the region and the orange and blue Utinsa buses run the routes in the south, but the coverage is by no means comprehensive.

WHERE TO STAY

Accommodation is sparse.

LUXURY
Hotel Bahía Mar,
Urbanización La Estrella, La Garita, Telde, tel: 928 130808, fax: 928 131960. Modern resort on the seafront with good sport facilities.

MID-RANGE
Hotel Golf de Bandama,
Ctra a Bandama s/n, tel: 928 353354, fax: 928 351290. A small,country-house hotel alongside Gran Canaria's earliest golf course.
Hotel Escuela Santa Brígida, C/Real de Coello 2, Santa Brígida, tel: 928 355511, fax: 928 355314. Good service at this country establishment that is also a training school for the hotel industry.

BUDGET
Residencia Tiempo Libro,
Camino a las Olivas 1, Santa Brígida, tel: 928 640450. One of a chain of hotels subsidized and run by the government.

WHERE TO EAT

The northern part of the area, particularly around Santa Brígida and the Tafiras, has a number of country restaurants. Many are quite expensive and very popular with the inhabitants of Las Palmas, particularly over weekends. Traditional Canarian food is widely available in this area.

LUXURY
Bentayga, Ctra del Centro, Santa Brígida, tel: 928 350245. A highly recommended restaurant with superb meat dishes.
Hotel Santa Brígida Escuela, Calle Real de Coello 2, Santa Brígida, tel: 928 355511. The hotel training school kitchen services this inspired restaurant.

MID-RANGE
Tagoror, Montaña los Tierras 21, Guayadeque, Agüimes, tel: 928 172058. A cave restaurant at the end of the Barranco de Guayadeque serving Canarian food.
La Pardilla, Calle Raimundo Lulio 54, La Pardilla, Telde, tel: 928 695102. Good traditional Canarian as well as international food on the sea side of the town.

BUDGET
Budget restaurants are scarce. **Tapas** bars, in the older central parts of the country towns, may be your best bet.

TOURS AND EXCURSIONS

The area is popular with half-day and full-day tours, which are organized by travel agents in the south. Tours are often combined with a morning's shopping in Las Palmas. The most popular excursion destinations are the **Caldera de Bandama**, the **Jardín Botánico Canario** and the **Barranco de Guayadeque**. Hotel receptions usually advise guests on excursions.

USEFUL CONTACTS

The only **tourist information office** in the area is a small-scale undertaking in Telde at Calle de Juan Carlos 1, just off the Plaza de San Juan.

5
The South

Tourists arriving at Gando airport and travelling south to their holiday destinations must first drive through the most unappealing part of Gran Canaria. The semiarid landscape is decorated with industrial estates, plastic greenhouses and wind farms, but fortunately things do improve as the **'Costa Canaria'** comes into view and the landscape now resembles the Gran Canaria of the holiday brochures. This is a purpose-built string of resorts, stretching from the relatively upmarket **San Agustín** in the east to **Mogán** in the west, which has been constructed over the last 40 years on what was largely a deserted stretch of coastline. Today it is a holiday conurbation, which centres on **Playa del Inglés** – which is a loud, lively gay resort with a lot of 'clubbers' – and **Maspalomas** – a more family-oriented resort – and it provides the visitor with everything from hotels and apartments to bars, discos, restaurants and sporting activities. Don't look for a shady square with an historic church or a traditional museum – they don't exist here. The area has numerous **theme parks** that are very popula,r ranging from bird parks and aqua parks to fun fairs and locations resembling the Wild West.

In the early years of development, buildings were hurriedly erected without considering the environment. More recently, environmental and visual considerations have resulted in more attractive developments, such as **Puerto de Mogán** in the west, where canals and flower-bedecked houses have led to the description, 'little Venice'. In the years to come there will undoubtedly be many battles between local environmentalists and greedy developers.

LAS PALMAS
DE GRAN CANARIA
Agaete • Arucas •
• Telde
San Nicolás   Pico de los
de Tolentino   Nieves
▲
1949 m
Puerto de Mogán
Maspalomas • • Playa del Inglés

DON'T MISS

*** Palmitos Park: the island's top theme park, set amongst an oasis of palms.
** The Dunes at Maspalomas: a vast area of sand dunes with a lagoon, oasis and camel rides.
** Puerto de Mogán: a harbour-side development described as little Venice.
* Sioux City: bank raids, gunfights and cattle runs at this Wild West theme park.
* Water Sports at Puerto Rico: a lively resort famous for its sailing and deep-sea fishing activities.

Opposite: *Part of the area of sand dunes near the resort of Maspalomas.*

Above: *The crowded, sandy beach at Playa del Inglés, Gran Canaria's most popular resort.*

THE EASTERN SECTION

The GC1 coastal motorway runs parallel to the C812, which passes the unattractive town of **Vecindario**. With the growth of tourism, the previously arid and sparsely populated coastal plain now has the largest towns. The administrative centre, which was once the mountain town of Santa Lucía de Tirajana, is now Vecindario. There are now signs of tourist developments in the areas where the side roads reach the sea. Windsurfing spots can be found at places such as **Pozo Izquierdo**, **Bahía Feliz** and **Playa del Águila**.

The major resort, **San Agustín**, was the first to be built and it still maintains a slightly more upmarket image than its neighbours to the west, due to the three prestigious hotels and their fine exotic gardens. Unfortunately, San Agustín is literally cut in half by the C812. Visitors staying north of the coast road face a long walk to the beach, but they are compensated with fine views. The dark sand beach at San Agustín stretches some 2km (1.2 miles). It is safe for bathing and offers numerous facilities for water sports.

Playa del Inglés

The liveliest and most popular resort on the island, **Playa del Inglés** has something for everyone. First impressions can be disappointing, as the resort appears to be a charmless sprawl of hotels and apartments without any attractive features. There are large commercial centres (*centros comerciales*) at convenient spots with several storeys of shops, bars, restaurants and clubs. Getting around the resort is easy; the taxis are cheap, there are regular buses and there is even a small "train" that travels along the roads. The beach is long and sandy, but usually crowded. Facilities are provided for various water sports, and sun beds and parasols can be hired. Alongside the beach is a coastal promenade, the **Paseo Costa Canario**, which stretches from the direction of San Agustín to that of Maspalomas. The **Ecumenical Church of San Salvador**, on Calle de Malaga, is intriguing with its huge arched façade resembling a cave entrance. There is plenty of accommodation in Playa del Inglés – there are 20 large hotels and over 250 apartment complexes. There is also an abundance restaurants to choose from, serving food from all over the world to suit every pocket. The focal point of the resort is the huge **Centro Yumbo**, a four-storeyed commercial complex built around a charming square. It includes many shops selling perfumes, electrical goods, books and clothing, as well as a vast selection of restaurants and bars. You will also find banks, doctors, internet cafés, supermarkets and launderettes. Discos, gay bars and

---

THE GODFATHER OF TOURISM

Forty years ago the arid southern coast of Grand Canaria was almost deserted, with only the occasional fishing village and one or two farmers scratching out a precarious living. Much of the land was owned by a count, **Conde de la Vega Grande**, who was a wealthy grandee with an influential and well established family. The count, who was based in Telde, found that his estates in the south of the island were of little financial use, so he decided to develop a tourist complex in what is now San Agustín. Playa del Inglés and Maspalomas soon followed, and the rest, as they say, is history.

night clubs open their doors in the late evening and the
excitement continues until dawn. The main tourist information centre for the area is located on the corner of the
Yumbo Centre. Playa del Inglés's football ground and
wrestling stadium are situated in the *barrio* **San
Fernando**, in the north of the town, where most of the
local employees live. This is a good place to buy cheap,
everyday groceries and it is also the best area to find
genuine *tapas* bars.

MASPALOMAS

Playa del Inglés merges with the more upmarket resort of
Maspalomas to the west. It has no high-rise buildings, as
it was built approximately 10 years after Playa del Inglés
and the architects were more environmentally conscious.
It consists mainly of villas and bungalow-type complexes
that are set around pools. There are plenty of areas that
have been left in a natural state and the roads are wide
and lined with trees. Tour operators have contributed to
the development of the resort and this is evident in the
names of avenues, such as Avenida del Touroperador
Thomson. Not a *calle* (road or street) in sight! In the centre

Opposite: *The Campo
de Golf at Maspalomas
with the rolling dunes
in the background.*

of the resort is the **Campo de Golf**, which is the only 18-hole golf course on the island. Holiday bungalows and garden apartments, that provide convenient accommodation for visiting golfers, surround the course. Visitors can use the driving range, hire clubs and book lessons.

Las Dunas de Maspalomas **

The most interesting part of the resort is the area of sand dunes, **Las Dunas de Maspalomas**, which cover some 328 hectares (810 acres), with some of the ridges rising to 10m (33ft) in height. Lines of camels cross the dunes with loads of visitors and the eastern end of the dunes is an unofficial nudist area. A tidal, reed-fringed lagoon, known as the *charca*, marks the western side of the dunes. It is a nature reserve and a breeding ground for birds such as the moorhen and the Kentish plover. Migrating sea birds and waders are also attracted to this area. The stone bank to the west of the *charca* is the home of some large Canarian lizards that are tame enough to photograph. Local environmentalists are fighting hard to prevent further tourist developments encroaching on to the dunes and the *charca*.

TIMESHARE TOUTS

One of the irritations of a holiday in Gran Canaria is the ubiquitous timeshare tout, who hangs around markets, promenades and other crowded places. Officially known as an off-property contact, his job is to entice visitors to a timeshare location with free gifts and special holiday offers. Here, hard-sell techniques are employed to persuade visitors to buy a share in a property in which they can take a holiday for one or two weeks a year for life. For some people the idea is attractive, but for many, especially those who like to visit a variety of holiday spots, it is unsuitable. The best advice is not to sign anything until you are sure of the financial implications and then take at least a week to reconsider your decision.

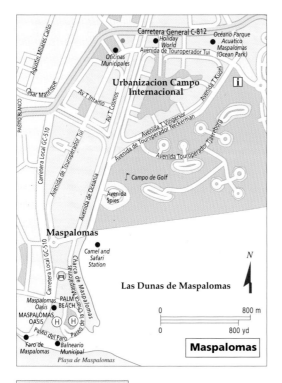

Maspalomas

The area to the west of the *charca* is lined with pretty palm trees and it has become well known as **El Oasis**. This small development has some exclusive bungalows and the Oasis Hotel has the most beautiful location of any hotel in the region. At the southern end of the complex is the **Faro de Maspalomas**, which – at a height of 65m (213ft) – is the highest lighthouse in the Canary Islands and marks the southernmost tip of Gran Canaria.

THEME PARKS AND OTHER ATTRACTIONS

When holidaymakers in the resorts of Playa del Inglés, Maspalomas and San Agustín favour a change to the beach or pool, or their children become restless, there are plenty of amusements just inland. Free shuttle coaches and regular bus services provide transport to theme parks and other attractions.

Sioux City *

This is in the Barranco del Aguila region, northwest of San Agustín. It is situated on an old western-style film set, forming the basis of an old cowboy town with wooden buildings, which include a bank, a bar, a prison and a sheriff's office. Gun fights and bank raids are enacted and skills such as knife throwing and lassoing are demonstrated. Visitors can ride a horse down the main street, have their photographs taken for a 'WANTED' poster and have a drink in the Last Chance Saloon. **Sioux**

JEEP SAFARIS

A good way to explore the countryside of Gran Canaria is by jeep safari. These vehicles can reach parts of the countryside – such as forest trails and rough volcanic terrain – which cannot be reached in cars. Remember that it can be hot, windy and uncomfortable and Gran Canaria has few mammals and only a small number of bird species. The scenery is, however, magnificent. Choose a reputable company with reliable vehicles.

City is open daily (10:00–17:00) and performances take place four times a day.

There are two water parks in the vicinity: **Océano Parque Acuatico Maspalomas** is right in the centre of Maspalomas, and **Aqua Sur** is located in the Barranco de Chamoriscán, north of the town. Both offer a variety of slides, wave pools, other amusements and restaurants, and they are open daily from 10:00 to 17:00.

Holiday World can be found at Campo Internacional next to the Océano Parque in Maspalomas. It is essentially a large funfair with Dodgems, swings, a lazerdrome and a giant Ferris wheel, which is a landmark for miles around. It is open from 10:00 to 17:00 daily. There are two **go-karting** locations – **Karting Maspalomas**, alongside Océano Parque, and the **Gran Karting Club** at Tarajalillo, just east of San Agustín. Both are open between 10:00 and 22:00, but they are expensive.

FERAL EXOTIC BIRDS

Although Gran Canaria has only a small number of breeding bird species, the escaped exotic birds compensate for this. Theme parks, such as Palmitos Parque, have large collections of foreign birds and it is inevitable that some of these escape. Indeed, many at Palmitos are encouraged to fly freely. The escapees find that in the benign climate of the Canary Islands they can find plenty of food and many are able to breed. Parrots, parakeets and lovebirds thrive on the island, and flocks of ring-necked parakeets are a common sight in Maspalomas. Even caged birds, such as zebra finches (from the Indian subcontinent), can be seen living in the wild.

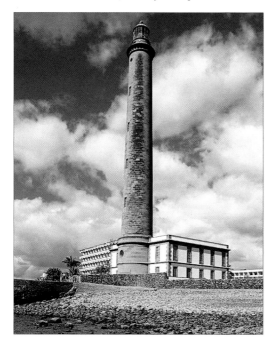

Left: *The Faro de Maspalomas is the tallest lighthouse in the Canary Islands and marks the southernmost tip of Gran Canaria.*

Palmitos Parque ★★★

Most visitors vote **Palmitos Parque** as their favourite
attraction in Gran Canaria. The park is a man-made
oasis at the head of the Barranco de Chamoriscán some
15km (9.3 miles) northwest of Playa de Inglés. It opened
in the 1970s and it has improved and enlarged consis-
tently ever since. The park is now the home of over 200
species of exotic birds such as flamingos, hornbills,
macaws, parrots, lovebirds and toucans. Many are free
to fly around the area and this explains the number of
parrots and similar birds that screech around the
rooftops of the coastal resorts. Paths wind around the
park through Canary palms, euphorbia, cacti and
colourful climbing plants. Several small ponds have
exotic wild fowl and a stream tumbles down the valley.
Recent innovations include an orchid house, a butterfly
garden and a superb aquarium with curved tanks set
against rock walls with tropical fish from many parts of
the world. A parrot show is performed seven times a
day where the birds stage tricks such as riding small

Left: *Lovebird at Palmitos Parque. This popular theme park has a wide range of birds, both in avaries and flying free.*
Opposite: *The cactus garden at Palmitos Parque. The park is generally considered to be Gran Canaria's most popular attraction.*

bicycles, walking tightropes, putting together jigsaw puzzles and even working out elementary sums! Palmitos Parque is open daily (09:00–18:00) and can be reached by shuttle buses from the southern resorts. Admission is pricey, but worth every euro. Note that the disabled might find some of the paths unaccommodating. Visitors who come to Palmitos Parque by car can climb to the head of the valley and return to the coast along a parallel road to the east.

Mundo Aborigen ★

This can best be described as an archaeological park. It is located on the hillslopes on the side of the Barranco de Fataga, some 6km (3.7 miles) north of Playa del Inglés. It has displays depicting the way the Guanche inhabitants of Gran Canaria lived in the days before the Spanish Conquest in the 15th century. A small village has been constructed with simple buildings and caves, and you can see life-sized figures cooking *gofio*, making craft items, carrying out trepanning operations and mummifying bodies. All the activities are explained in English, German and Spanish. There are occasional shows demonstrating stick fighting, pole vaulting, wrestling and other Guanche accomplishments. The whole site covers more than 100,000 square metres of a typical Guanche territory and the visitor leaves with a lasting impression of the way these Stone Age people lived. **Mundo Aborigen** is open daily (09:00–18:00). The Barranco de Fataga is also the site of **Manolo's Camel**

USEFUL VOLCANIC CINDERS

The rock materials from the extinct volcanoes on Gran Canaria have been fully utilized by the inhabitants of the island from the time of the Guanches to the present day. Weathered down volcanic **ash** makes a very fertile soil, while the hard **basalt** is an excellent building stone. More unusually, **lapilli** (volcanic cinders) make a useful mulch material for market gardens and flowerbeds, such as those in hotel gardens. The cinders trap the moisture from mist and at the same time they prevent the loss of moisture through evaporation in sunny weather. In addition, the cinders prevent the growth of weeds.

Right: *Camel safaris are enjoyed on the sand dunes at Maspalomas.*

Safaris and **Camel Safari La Baranda**, where one can experience camel rides similar to those in Maspalomas.

THE WEST OF THE REGION

The coastline on the west of Maspalomas consists of a series of mainly small developments interspersed with arid slopes and rocky headlands.

If travelling in this direction, look for the white towers and domes of the **Estación de Siguimiento** and **Estación Espacial NASA** – the NASA Space Tracking Station – located on the right-hand side of the GC1 motorway. Almost immediately opposite, a minor road leads down to **Pasito Blanco**. This is a complex of houses positioned around a busy marina, occupied by yachts and sport-fishing boats.

Both the C812 and the motorway lead to the small town of **Arguineguín**. This is the end of the motorway and there are no plans to extend it further in this direction. There are frequent tailbacks at this point of the motorway, particularly at the height of the tourist season. A small part of this fishing port is being developed, but the ugly cement works make the place unattractive to visitors. One spot worth finding, however, is the harbour-side seafood restaurant, the *Cofradia de Pescadores*, run by the local fishermen's co-operative, where fresh food is guaranteed. Arguineguín is linked to its neighbour, **Patalavaca** (the name means cow's hoof), by a coastal promenade. There has been more development in Patalavaca, due to its decent sandy beach.

WHALE AND DOLPHIN WATCHING

Visitors on boat trips around the shores of Gran Canaria are often lucky enough to see dolphins swimming or leaping out of the water alongside the vessel. The species most usually seen are the **common dolphin** (*Delphinus delphis*) and the **bottlenose dolphin** (*Tursiops truncates*). Travellers may also be lucky enough to see whales, which are often spotted from inter-island ferries. A large colony of **short-finned pilot whales** (*Globicephala macrorhynchus*) are often seen in the waters between Gran Canaria and Tenerife. There is also a healthy population of **sperm whales** (*Physeter macrocephalus*), which can grow up to 18m (59ft) in length and weigh up to 60 tons.

Puerto Rico *

The scenery now changes and the coastal road that runs along the top of steep cliffs provides superb sea views in each direction, before descending into **Puerto Rico**. This is the least attractive resort on Gran Canaria. A *barranco* widens out to meet the sea at this point and stark white, low-rise apartment blocks cover the hill slopes, so that there is scarcely room for another building. Visitors staying at apartments on the hill face a long walk to the beach and back. There is a public park, a commercial centre and a water park along the bottom of the valley.

NUDE SUNBATHING

Topless sunbathing is common on beaches and around hotel and apartment pools. Full nudity, however, is offensive to *Canarios*. There are, nevertheless, beaches where nudity is tolerated. The best known location is the dune area of Maspalomas, just west of Playa del Inglés. Be careful, as these areas sometimes attract voyeurs and deviant types.

SAFE SWIMMING

Keen swimmers are well catered for in Gran Canaria. All hotels and even the humblest apartment blocks have a pool, although they are often not heated and the water can be very cold in winter. Aqua parks are also found near the southern resorts, although many visitors wish to swim in the Atlantic. The island does have some excellent beaches and the most popular beaches meet European Blue Flag standards and many have lifeguards in attendance. Care should be taken near rocks and on beaches in remote areas. It is also sensible to find out whether there are dangerous currents and undertows.

Left: *The resort of Puerto Rico has a thriving water sports harbour and a very busy sandy beach.*

DEEP-SEA FISHING

Visitors wishing to try their hand at deep-sea game fishing have plenty of opportunity in the south of Gran Canaria. The marinas at Puerto de Mogán, Puerto Rico and Pasito Blanco all hire out boats and all the necessary equipment to small groups of anglers. The usual fish caught here include marlin, swordfish and tuna. Some boats specialize in shark fishing, particularly those from Puerto Rico. Make reservations early to avoid disappointment.

Below: *The tasteful coastal village of Puerto de Mogán has been described as Gran Canaria's little Venice.*

The valley opens out onto a broad beach of imported sand. Breakwaters make this a safe beach for swimming and the resort has become very popular with families. There is a busy yachting harbour with a sailing school at the western end of the beach. Proud sailors from Puerto Rico have provided Spain with a number of Olympic medals in recent years and some of the roads in the town have been named after them. A smaller harbour, **Puerto Nuevo**, has recently been built at the eastern end of the beach. Puerto Rico's other claim to fame is that it is the island's main centre for deep-sea fishing and its boats have achieved several world records. Marlin, swordfish and tuna are the most common of the fish that are caught here. Other water sports available at Puerto Rico include sail boarding and waterskiing.

The coast road becomes even more exciting just west of Puerto Rico. It hugs the cliff edge and occasionally drops down at the mouths of *barrancos* where there are small modern developments such as **Taurito**, **Tauro** and **Playa del Cura**.

Puerto de Mogán ★★

After the garish developments further east, Puerto de Mogán is a pleasant surprise. It is based on a small but lively fishing village. The tourist development that has been added onto it has been described as one of the island's finest projects and a superb example of what can be done without spoiling the environment. The once

Above: *The famous Yellow Submarine based at Puerto de Mogán.*

modest fishing harbour has been expanded in order to accommodate an armada of luxury boats and yachts waiting for the right conditions to cross the Atlantic. Behind the harbour is a neat complex of white, two-storeyed buildings dripping with bougainvillea and hibiscus. These buildings are intersected with canals and attractive arched bridges. This traffic-free area is often described as little Venice. Small alleyways and squares with wrought iron street lamps and shady palm trees complete the picture. The fishermen's quarter, just up the hill, has a unique atmosphere and it is well worth a visit. The small beach made of imported sand offers safe swimming for visitors. Puerto de Mogán attracts many visitors from the larger resorts further east. Most arrive by car and coach, but it is possible to take the boat that links Arguineguín, Puerto Rico and Puerto de Mogán and which runs several times a day. A popular attraction at Puerto de Mogán is the **Yellow Submarine**, a genuine submersible in which travellers have their own porthole to view fish and old wrecks. There is a bus that runs between here and the main resorts at no charge.

Accommodation at Puerto de Mogán is largely confined to small *pensions* and privately rented apartments.

> **WATER SPORTS**
>
> The resorts in southern Gran Canaria offer just about every conceivable type of water sport, ranging from pedalos, banana boats, parascending and jet skiing, to more skilful activities such as sailing, scuba diving, waterskiing and windsurfing. Note that the northern part of the island is probably better for surfing. All water sports can be dangerous and swimmers should beware of underwater rocks and strong currents. Do not underestimate the strength of the prevailing winds, which are at their strongest in the afternoon and can provide problems for novices.

The South at a Glance

BEST TIMES TO VISIT

Lying in the rain shadow of the central mountains, the south of Gran Canaria is an all-year-round destination because of its almost unbroken sunshine. Tourists from northern Europe visit in the winter months, while in the summer, mainland Spaniards find the area is not as oppressively hot as it is in the peninsula. If there are any off-peak periods at all, they are in **May/June** and **October/November**, and this is the most opportune time to make last-minute bookings.

GETTING THERE

The south is easily reached from Gando Airport via the GC1 motorway and the C812 coastal road. Salcai **buses** run at regular intervals from the airport to the major resorts. **Taxis** can be hired from the airport and are relatively cheap in comparison to mainland Europe. All the main international **car hire** agencies have offices at Gando airport and their rates are amongst the cheapest in Europe. Playa del Inglés and Maspalomas can be reached within half an hour from the airport. Remember, however, that the motorway ends at Arguineguín, so it takes longer to travel to the western resorts.

GETTING AROUND

A hired **car** is an asset, especially with the reasonable rates and inexpensive petrol. The coastal roads are in good

condition, but motorists should be aware that inland roads can be narrow, have numerous hairpin bends and can degenerate into dirt tracks. A good map is useful. **Taxis** are cheap and widely used for local journeys. Salcai **buses** run frequently between the coastal resorts. Free shuttle buses run from the resorts to the theme parks, such as Palmitos Parque and Aqua Sur.

WHERE TO STAY

In the area from San August in to Maspalomas there are 22 hotels and over 300 apartment blocks and bungalow complexes. Clearly most visitors prefer to self-cater. Anyone planning to stay in the south of the island should not just turn up and expect to find a bed – nearly all accommodation is prebooked. If there are vacancies, the local Tourist Information Centre should have details. Some apartments, particularly those built in early years, are neglected and in need of refurbishment.

LUXURY

Maspalomas Oasis, Plaza de las Palmeras 2, Maspalomas, tel: 928 141448, fax: 928 141192. Large hotel near the *charca* and dunes.
Palm Beach, Avda del Oasis s/n, Maspalomas, tel: 928 140806, fax: 928 141808. Large luxury hotel with excellent facilities.
Dunamar, Avda Helsinki 8,

Playa del Inglés, tel: 928 772800, fax: 928 773465. On the beach, with good leisure facilities.
Meliá Tamarindos, Calle Las Retamas 3, San Augustin, tel: 928 774090, fax: 928 774091. Luxury hotel in a quiet location, with a casino.

MID-RANGE

Club de Mar, Castillete s/n, Puerto de Mogán, tel: 928 565066. An apartment block with a few hotel facilities by the sports harbour.
Continental, Avenida del Italia 2, Playa del Inglés, tel: 928 760033, fax: 928 771484. Good family hotel close to the beach.
Sun Club Playa del Inglés, Avda Francia 13, Playa del Inglés, tel: 928 762870. Good standard apartments at the western end of the resort.
Campo de Golf, Avenida Neckerman, Maspalomas, tel: 928 762582. Accommodation surrounding a golf course.

BUDGET

Molino de Fataga, Ctra.de Fataga a San Bartoleme km 1, tel: 928 172089. Small rural hotel in a converted *gofio* mill.
Inter Club Atlantic, Los Jazmines 2, San Agustin, tel: 928 760950, fax: 928 760974. Good sport facilities and pool.
Los Tilos, Adva España 11, Playa del Inglés, tel: 928 773908. Reasonably priced apartments close to the Centro Yumbo.

The South at a Glance

There are only three official **camp sites** on Gran Canaria and two are in the south; near Puerto de Mogán there is **Camping Guantanamo**, Playa Tauro, tel: 928 560207, which is a well-equipped site with plenty of shade, and there is another camp site at **Pasito Blanco** just next to the Marina.

WHERE TO EAT

San Agustín, Playa del Inglés and Maspalomas offer many restaurants serving international food. Some serve typical Canarian food and others dish up superb seafood, especially the restaurants in the old fishing ports such as Arguineguín and Puerto de Mogán.

LUXURY
La Toja, Avda Tirajana 17, Playa del Inglés, tel: 928 761196. One of the best fish restaurants in the south, offering both French and Galician cuisine.
Amaiur, Avda Neckerman, Maspalomas, tel: 928 764414. Superb Basque cooking.
Acayama, Calle Tostador, Mogán, tel: 928 569263. Considered to be one of the finest restaurants in Gran Canaria.

MID-RANGE
Cofradía de Pescadores, Avda De Muelle s/n, Arguineguín, tel: 928 150963. Fresh seafood at

the fishermen's co-operative on the quayside. There is a similar restaurant on the harbour-side at Puerto de Mogán.
El Faro, Puerto de Mogán, tel: 928 565373. Fresh seafood in this old lighthouse at the end of the quay.
Bali, Avda Tirajana 23, Playa del Inglés. Serving classic Indonesian food.
Pepe el Breca, Ctra de Fataga, Maspalomas, tel: 928 772637. One of the best spots in the south for traditional Canarian food.

BUDGET
Finding budget food in the main resorts of the south is easy, as there are plenty of pizza outlets and branches of American fast food chains such as McDonalds and KFC. Chinese restaurants, too, can provide inexpensive meals. Many restaurants providing international food will have a *menu del día* with three courses at a bargain price. Playa del Inglés also has a number of *buffet libre* restaurants where you can eat as much food as you like for a set price. A good example here is **Tropicana** in the Centro Yumbo (a very large centre occupying an entire block), which also has live music. Genuine *tapas* bars are few, although there are some in the *barrio* of San Fernando, a district of Playa del Inglés just north of the motorway.

TOURS AND EXCURSIONS

Local tour operators run coach excursions all over the island. The most popular destinations are the **Barranco de Guayadeque** – which usually involves a typical Canarian meal and some folk music – and shopping excursions to **Las Palmas** that are often combined with visits to the **Caldera de Bandama** or the **Jardín Botánico**. Other trips, particularly in the form of **jeep safaris**, take in the mountain scenery in the centre of the island. There are also boat trips along the coast such as the windjammer *San Miguel*, which operates from Puerto Rico, and the large luxury motor boat run by **Lineas Salmon**, which has regular trips that link Arguineguín, Puerto Rico and Puerto de Mogán. **Travel Agents** in Playa del Inglés who arrange tours include Canary Travel, tel: 928 774712 and **Suntourist**, tel: 928 766489. **Miguel's Jeep** tours are located at the Eurocentre, tel: 928 764896.

USEFUL CONTACTS

There are **tourist information offices** at **Playa del Inglés** next to the Yumbo Centre in Avda de España, tel: 928 767848, open from Monday to Friday (09:00–21:00) and Saturday (09:00–14:00), and in **Puerto Rico** the tourist information office is in the main shopping centre, tel: 928 560029.

6
The West

The western side of the island of Gran Canaria is one of its most sparsely populated regions. There are just three small towns: **Mogán** in the south, and **San Nicolás de Tolentino** and **Agaete** – with its port **Puerto de las Nieves** – in the north. In between these towns the mountainous region is virtually uninhabited. There are some *barrancos* with fertile soil in the bottom of the valleys, but many farmers have moved to the resorts where there is a lot more profitable work. Many hamlets have become depopulated and those who have remained behind are usually the elderly.

The west has also resisted tourist development. Plans have been put forward at **Playa de Veneguera** and **Playa de la Aldea** and there have been furious objections from environmentalists, although many local people would welcome the employment that such developments would offer.

The west provides Gran Canaria's most majestic coastal scenery. Cliffs, small boulder-strewn coves and imposing headlands, grace the coastline. In the northwest, the coastal route is known as the **Anden Verde** (or Green Platform) and here there are some corniche roads providing exciting driving, especially when passing a local bus on a narrow bend. Coastal vistas are spectacular, with the best viewpoint at the **Mirador del Balcón** – a cliff-top viewing platform just a few kilometres north of **San Nicolás de Tolentino**.

The transport infrastructure in the west is minimal. The main road through the area is the C810 and there are

LAS PALMAS DE GRAN CANARIA
Agaete
Arucas
San Nicolás de Tolentino
Pico de los Nieves
▲ 1949 m
•Telde
Puerto de Mogán
Maspalomas • •Playa del Inglés

DON'T MISS

** **Mirador del Balcón:** a platform providing exquisite views of the west coast and Mount Teide on Tenerife.
** **Puerto de las Nieves:** experience the finest seafood on the island.
* **Dedo de Dios:** remarkable sea stack known as the 'Finger of God'.
* **Playa de Veneguera:** secluded beach – enjoy it before it is developed.

Opposite: *The pebble-strewn beach at Puerto de las Nieves is popular with weekenders from Las Palmas.*

only two minor roads that lead from this route into the interior. One runs inland just north of Mogán and the other is a gravel road from San Nicolás. Both of these roads are popular with jeep safaris.

THE MOGÁN VALLEY

At **Puerto de Mogán**, the coastal road leaves the tourist resorts and stretches inland where the scenery abruptly changes. Initially the C810 runs along the **Barranco de Mogán**, a broad valley with a succession of small hamlets surrounded by fields growing subtropical fruits such as bananas, papayas and mangos. The roadside here is decorated with unique sculptures made from old household implements, and dominating the view is a restored windmill, which was once used to ground the grain to make *gofio*.

Before long, you arrive at the little town of **Mogán**. This pleasant place is the administrative centre for much of the southwest of the island. It has attracted a number of writers and artists in recent years and, with its abundance of water, Mogán is distinguished by its luxuriant gardens. There are some rather expensive restaurants in the town, but there are also markets, hiking trails and a few areas of

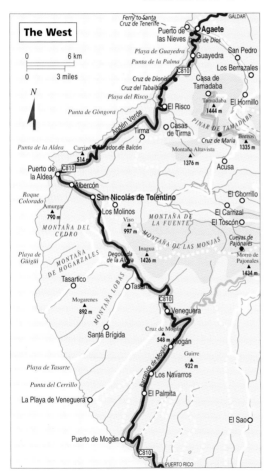

The West

0   6 km
0   3 miles
N

historic interest to detain the visitor. The road makes a sharp turn to the left, just north of Mogán, and on the bend a minor road follows a tortuous route into the interior of the island. This passes a number of reservoirs, including both the **Embalse del Mulato** and the **Embalse de la Cueva de las Niñas** (the Cave of the Little Girls), and with its picturesque picnic spots, it is a favourite route for jeep safaris.

Veneguera *

After some intimidating hairpin bends, a road to the left leads to the sleepy hamlet of **Veneguera**. From here a dirt track runs down the *barranco* for 8km (5 miles) to **La Playa de Veneguera**. The track is only suitable for four-wheel-drive vehicles and this ensures that the dark sand beach remains secluded. In 1990, however, permission was granted to the Spanish bank, Banesto, to develop the area so that it would be able to accommodate over 20,000 holidaymakers. Playa de Veneguera is in a conservation area, so anger from local environmentalists has put the development on hold. A road is being built linking Playa de Veneguera with Puerto de Mogán and it seems it might only be a matter of time before this idyllic spot joins the string of resorts along the south-west coast of the island.

The area known as **Los Azulejos** can be seen from the side of the main road. The word translates as 'tiles' in Spanish and it refers to the brightly coloured volcanic rocks that resemble the ceramic tiles found in Spanish homes, on seats and around fountains. Here, bright colours are seen at the side of the road where bands of volcanic ash have been exposed. The layers have been stained blue and green by the minerals, particularly

Above: *Los Azulejos – layers of coloured volcanic rock named after the beautiful ceramic tiles found in Spanish homes.*

CLIMATE

The weather in the west varies considerably. In the south of the area, around Mogán, the climate is similar to the resorts along the coast – hot in the summer and warm in the winter with little rain. Along the west coast, the weather is a lot wetter, particularly in winter, and the land is greener. The lowland around Agaete in the north is somewhat drier, and be prepared for coastal mist in the winter months.

iron and copper, which are found in the volcanic rocks. A roadside café with wonderful views makes this a popular stop.

Tasarte and Tasartico

As the road continues towards San Nicolás, there are two more side roads to the left that can take more intrepid visitors to coastal coves. The first leads to the hamlet of **Tasarte** and a gravel track leads further down the steep-sided Barranco de Tasarte, where there are small patches of cultivated land, to the Playa de Tasarte. Here, there is a small beach bar that is especially popular with the locals over weekends. Swimming in this area is safe, but this beach does not have as much potential for development as Veneguera to the south. The second road runs to Artejévez and then loops back to the main road. Further along the main road, another *barranco* leads to the hamlet of **Tasartico** and eventually to the Playa de Tasartico. The beach here is rather rocky and despite plans to build a new road, the area seems inappropriate for development. As the main highway approaches San Nicolás, a parallel minor road passes through the village of **Tocodomán**, where a cactus garden – reputed to have over two million specimens – is the centre of attraction.

SAN NICOLÁS DE TOLENTINO

The road now descends into a fertile valley, Valle del Barranco de Aldea, with numerous windmills. In the centre of the valley is the market town of **San Nicolás de Tolentino**. A variety of crops are grown here, including tomatoes, potatoes and cucumber, as well as tropical fruits such as bananas and oranges. Much of the produce is grown under plastic, which covers large areas of the valley floor. The tomato trade has suffered a lot in recent years, particularly with its competition from Morocco, and this has contributed to the migration of many of the local inhabitants, both to other parts of the island and overseas. Despite the age of the town (it is one of the oldest on the island) it has few tourist attractions. To the east of San Nicolás, a minor road runs up the *barranco* and climbs into the interior. It runs alongside a string of reservoirs, including the **Embalse Caidero de la Niña**, the **Embalse de Siberio** and the **Embalse de Parralillo**, and eventually reaches the mountain town of Artenara.

In the opposite direction the main road runs down to the coast, where there is the small fishing settlement of **Puerto San Nicolás** (or Puerto de la Aldea). To the south is the **Playa de la Aldea** (the town beach), which is quite desolate, boulder-strewn and backed by scrub and pine trees, with a small lagoon at the far end. There seems little chance of the area developing as a tourist centre, despite the hopes of the locals.

Opposite: *San Nicolás lies in the fertile Aldea valley, where many subtropical fruits, such as bananas and oranges, are grown under plastic.*
Below: *The coastal view from the Mirador del Balcón. Mount Teide, on the island of Tenerife, can usually be seen if the weather is clear.*

Mirador del Balcón **

The C810 ascends out of the valley and heads northwards, rendering fine views over the town, the plasticultura as well as the central mountains. The area holding the most magnificent coastal scenery on Gran Canaria, known as Anden Verde (Green Platform), is nearby. The corniche road demands the driver's full concentration, although there are a few places where it is possible to stop and take in the view. An exceptional view-

COLOURFUL VOLCANIC MATERIAL

Although it has been many centuries since volcanic activity occurred on Gran Canaria, the legacy of these eruptions is evident all over the island. The colourful layers of volcanic ash seen in many parts of Gran Canaria, such as Los Azulejos near Mogán, is a manifestation of this. Volcanic material usually becomes lighter with age, but here the ash appears in striking colours. The rocks owe their colours to their **mineral content**; iron stains the ash brown and red, while copper produces the green and blue tints.

point is at the Mirador del Balcón, where there is a small parking area and steps lead down to a viewing platform. From here you can see vistas stretching right along to the north end of the island, with volcanic cliffs several hundred metres in height and the Atlantic waves crashing at their base. In the distance towards the west, the island of Tenerife is usually identifiable, with the volcano of **Mount Teide** rising 3718m (12,200ft) above the mist and clouds. Take a close look at the surface of the ocean, where dolphins, and occasionally whales, may be seen. Further north, the **Pinar de Tamadaba Natural Park** bounds the road in the east. You cannot gain access to the park from the coastal road – it has to be reached from Artenara and the centre of the island. The only settlement along the Anden Verde is the little hamlet of **El Risco**, where a roadside restaurant, which makes its own bread, is a convenient stop.

AGAETE AND THE PUERTO DE LAS NIEVES

After a further series of hairpin bends the coastal road descends suddenly into the mouth of the Agaete *barranco*. The town of **Agaete** is a pleasant enough place, with narrow alleyways and buildings that have been looked after. An interesting feature is the 19th-century **Iglesia de la Concepción**, distinguished by its small, red dome. Inside are two parts of a 16th-century Flemish triptych (the third section is in the *ermita* (hermitage) in Puerto de las Nieves). Very close to the church is the **Huerto de las Flores** – a shady botanical garden, where the poet Tomás Morales wrote some of his best works. The gardens, which have some rare trees and both tropical and Canarian plants, are open during the mornings from 08:00 to 12:00. Southeast of Agaete, a road – signposted 'El Valle' – runs through the

Below: *The market town of Agaete, the largest settlement on the west coast of Gran Canaria.*

fertile *barranco*, past groves of bananas, mangos, oranges and avocados, and sheltered by Canary palms. At the end of the valley, where the palms are replaced by the Canary pine, the road rises up to the little settlement of **Los Berrazales**. Here there was once a thriving spa resort with thermal baths. The spa buildings have fallen into disrepair, but the mineral waters, which are bottled and sold, can be sampled at the local hotel.

Above: *One of the many seafood restaurants in the fishing and ferry port of Puerto de las Nieves.*

Puerto de las Nieves **

Down the valley from Agaete is the little fishing port of **Puerto de las Nieves** (Port of the Snows) named not after the chilly form of precipitation, but the Virgen de las Nieves, the patron saint of fishermen. Although house-wives can be seen selling fresh fish at the roadside, the local fishing fleet has been reduced to about 50 boats. There are, however, a number of superb seafood restaurants located on the harbourside, which attract hordes of people from Las Palmas who stream across the north of the island over weekends. Puerto de las Nieves was once a busy port used to export local agricultural produce, but this trade has also dwindled in recent years. The port bustles with activity when the ferry from Tenerife arrives.

THE BAJADA DE LA RAMA

On an island where fiestas are a way of life, one of the most extraordinary celebrations is the **Bajada de la Rama** (the Procession of the Branches). It takes place at **Agaete** and **Puerto de las Nieves** on 4 August each year, when the inhabitants gather fresh branches from the mountains and walk down to the harbour in a procession and beat the waves with their branches. The ceremony is probably of pagan origin and was possibly an ancient rain ritual. After the whipping of the waves has taken place, traditional dancing, singing and celebrating continues.

Above: *There are many attractive houses in Puerto de las Nieves.*

Dedo de Dios *

There are two notable attractions in Puerto de las Nieves; one is the **Dedo de Dios** (Finger of God), a jagged narrow pinnacle that juts out of the sea, located just south of the town. It is a challenging subject for photographers, as under most conditions of light it blends with the cliffs in the background. The other attraction is the **Ermita de Nuestra Señora de las Nieves**, which dates from the 16th century and has some superb *Mudéjar* carvings. The chapel's most important feature is a 16th-century Flemish triptych, believed to be the work of Joos van Cleve (1485–1540) depicting the Virgin of the Snows. Both the nave and the room behind the altar are festooned with model sailing and motor ships, reminding the visitor of the port's maritime history. Finding the *ermita* open is something of a challenge. Your best bet is on Sundays and public holidays between 11:00 and 13:00, and on Saturday evenings during mass. Puerto de las Nieves has a small, black shingle beach and a few low-rise apartments, but it has seen little in the way of major tourist developments, although this could change in the near future.

The West at a Glance

BEST TIMES TO VISIT

The west of Gran Canaria is an all-year-round destination. The higher parts attract a certain amount of low cloud and rain during the winter months and sea mist can also make driving difficult at this time. The best advice is to choose a sunny day with good visibility, whatever the season, to visit this part of the island.

GETTING THERE

Ferries operated by the Fred Olsen Line run from Santa Cruz de Tenerife four times a day and arrive at Puerto de las Nieves. Utinsa **buses** run from Las Palmas to Agaete. **Coach** tours journey to the area from the main resorts in the south of the island. Many visitors reach the area by **hired car**.

GETTING AROUND

Local **bus** services are sparse, but Utinas's No. 101 links Agaete with San Nicolás de Tolentino. Four daily Salcai buses link the southern resorts with Mogán and then go on to Agaete. A **hired car** is undoubtedly the best way to get around the west, but be aware that the road crossing the area is narrow with many dangerous bends.

WHERE TO STAY

Accommodation is scarce in the western part of Gran Canaria, due to the lack of major resorts. The following covers almost every possibility:

Agaete
MID-RANGE
Casa Romantica, Valle de Agaete km 3.5, Agaete, tel: 928 898084. Better known as a restaurant, this rural establishment now offers rooms.

BUDGET
Apartamentos El Angosto, Camino el Angosto s/n, Agaete, tel: 928 898010. Self-catering option.

San Nicolás de Tolentino
BUDGET
Hotel Los Cascajos, Calle de los Cascajos 9, San Nicolás de Tolentino, tel: 928 891165. The only option, although simpler accommodation is available for budget travellers.

Mogán
Although there is no official accommodation in Mogán, a number of private houses advertise bed and breakfast. You can contact the tourist information office for details or just look out for the word *camas* (rooms) in windows. There are no **camp sites** or **youth hostels** in this area.

WHERE TO EAT

A few restaurants are recommended along the west coast, especially in the Agaete and Puerto de las Nieves area, where the seafood is fresh and appetizing. In the south there are a handful of restaurants at Mogán, but these tend to be expensive. Note

that there is only one roadside restaurant, the **Bar Perdomo** (at El Risco), between San Nicolás and Agaete.

Agaete and Puerto de las Nieves
MID-RANGE
Seafood restaurants are found all along the beach and harbour. One of the best is:
Bar-Restaurante El Dedo del Dios, right on the beach at Puerto de las Nieves, tel: 928 898000. Superb fresh seafood at reasonable prices, plus a view of the 'Finger of God'. In Agaete, the restaurants place more emphasis on Canarian country cooking:
Los Papayeros, Calle Alcade Armas Galván 22, tel: 928 898046. Very good country stews.
Casa Románitica, Valle de Agaete km 3.5, tel: 928 898084. International and Spanish food served.

Mogán
MID-range
Grill Acaymo, Calle El Tostador 14, Mogán, tel: 928 569263. Traditional restaurant with a terrace, serving Canarian food.

TOURS AND EXCURSIONS

Tour operators in the large southern resorts often run **coach tours** along the west coast. The main stops include **Los Azulejos**, the **Mirador del Balcón** and the **Dedo de Dios**, and often **Reptilandia**.

7
The Central Highlands

Many of the visitors to Gran Canaria arrive at Gando Airport and transfer to their hotels at resorts such as Maspalomas or Playa del Inglés, where they remain for the whole of their stay. They see nothing more of the island and this is a mistake, because just a few kilometres inland there is some of the best scenery that the Canary Islands has to offer. In order to explore the interior of Gran Canaria you can book a coach excursion or, better still, hire a car and travel independently.

The centre of the island is of volcanic origin and the mountains rise to nearly 2000m (6562ft). Volcanic activity ceased around 3000 years ago and erosion and vegetation have softened the remaining features, such as the calderas and lava flows. Some volcanic spines still remain – these are the cores of volcanoes, which have remained while the softer ashes around them have worn away. Two spectacular examples are **Roque Nublo** – the second highest peak on the island, standing at 1813m (5948ft) – and the 1412m (4633ft) **Roque Bentaiga**. These conspicuous crags can be seen from many places in the interior of the island.

The numerous *barrancos* (deeply incised valleys) – that run out from the centre of the island like the spokes of a wheel – were formed by rivers in wetter climatic conditions, but they are now mainly dry. The valley floors and terraced sides are widely cultivated areas; oranges, mangoes and subtropical fruits grow on the valley floors, while the terraces are lined with delicate white-blossomed almond trees that are picturesque in early spring. The mountainous centre of Gran Canaria

DON'T MISS

*** Artenara: Gran Canaria's highest village, dominated by a hilltop statue of Christ and many cave houses.
* Roque Nublo and Roque Bentaiga: see old volcanic spines, forming landmarks for miles around.
* Tamadaba Natural Park: a remote forest area ideal for camping or picnics.
* Fortaleza Grande: a natural rock castle, the last refuge of the Guanches.

Opposite: *The Statue of Christ in the village of Artenara.*

Opposite: *The pretty
village of Tejeda, amidst
the stunning scenery of
the Central Highlands.*

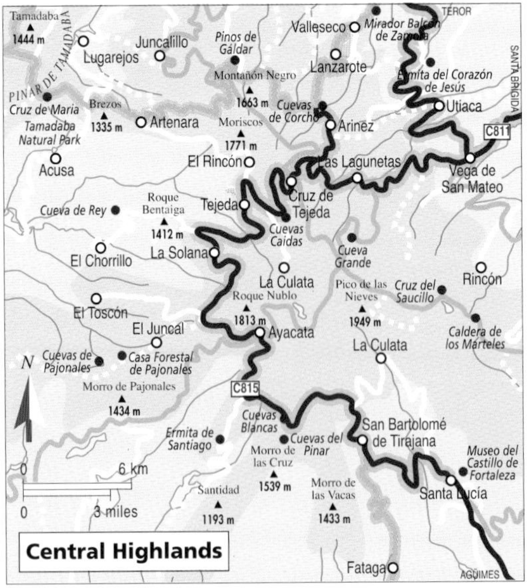

was the last stronghold of the **Guanches** in their resistance to the Spanish invaders. The last battle took place
at **Fortaleza Grande**, a castle-like crag of rock near Santa
Lucía. Here is much evidence of the caves where the
Guanches lived and kept their grain and animals. Even
today, there are numerous examples of occupied 'cave
houses' on the hillsides of highland villages. Among the
attractive villages in the area are **Tejeda**, famous for its
almond confectionery, and **Artenara**, which is the highest settlement on the island – lying at 1219m (4000ft)
above sea level.

Visitors who have hired a car to see the centre of the
island should be patient and wait for a cloud-free day
before embarking on a trip. Drivers should remember
that the roads of the interior are often narrow and there
are frequent hairpin bends. Travelling can be slow, so
allow plenty of time to take in the magnificent sights.
The lack of accurate signposts can also be frustrating, so
take along a good road map.

Central Highlands

ROUTES INTO THE CENTRAL HIGHLANDS

There are five routes – one
from Las Palmas, two
from the north and two
from the south. A couple
of tracks offer views of
some of the most attrac-
tive reservoirs, but these
should only be attempted
with four-wheel-drive
vehicles.

Vega de San Mateo

The journey from Las
Palmas follows the C811
through the **Tafiras** and
Santa Brígida before it
reaches the fertile plain of
the **Vega de San Mateo**.

On the *vega* (fertile plain) a wide variety of crops are grown including almonds, figs, pears and peaches. The main market town of the plain is **San Mateo**, which has a well known *romeria* in September. The Sunday morning market, which takes places in two large hangars on the outskirts of the town, is interesting to explore. As well as local produce, there are plenty of crafts on sale. The village church, fittingly, has a 17th-century statue of San Mateo, the patron saint of farmers. Near the entrance to the village is the **Casa Museo Cho' Zacarias**, a private museum located in an old roadside farmhouse. Its displays illustrate the rural life of the island and there are many examples of domestic utensils and farm implements. The museum is well worth a visit. It is open from Monday to Saturday (09:30–13:00).

Surrounding Attractions ★

The C811 eventually reaches **Cruz de Tejeda** at the central crossroads in the highlands. There are two routes into the interior from the north. The route on the west

---

VOLCANIC ROCKS

Although volcanic activity ceased over 3000 years ago, the rocks formed during this period can be seen everywhere in the Central Highlands. The hot material within a volcano is known as **magma**. When a volcano erupts, magma pours out of the volcano and it takes a number of forms. The liquid material is known as **lava** and it flows over long distances. The most common form of lava on Gran Canaria is **basalt**, which cools in distinctive columns. Explosive activity creates **ash**, which can form thick layers, and volcanic **bombs** which are called **pyroclasts**.

BARRANCOS

Gran Canaria had a much wetter climate in the recent geological past. The main evidence for this is the existence of *barrancos*. These are deep, steep-sided valleys, which radiate out from the centre of the island like the spokes of a wheel (geographers call this **radial drainage**). They were formed by streams, but today the *barrancos* are dry and Gran Canaria has no permanently flowing rivers.

passes Moya and Firgas, while the more easterly route begins at Arucas. The two roads meet near Teror and then proceed as the GC110 past the Mirador Balcón de Zamora and through the villages of **Valleseco** and **Lanzarote** to Cruz de Tejeda.

Visitors staying in the southern resorts have a choice between two routes. The most convenient leaves Playa del Inglés via the suburb of San Fernando and follows the attractive **Barranco de Fataga** northwards. Shortly, to the left, replica stone huts from Guanche times depict the open-air museum of **Mundo Arborigen** (*see page 91*). Just after this, there is a *mirador*, with restaurant, offering stunning views of the coast. The road now reaches the little village of **Fataga**, beautifully situated on a steep cliff reaching into the valley and surrounded by fertile terraces. Although Fataga has no ancient monuments of note, its alleyways, cobbled little squares and flower-filled patios reward a stroll. Camel safaris can be experienced just outside the village and although this form of transport is an acquired taste, you could not wish to be surrounded by more beautiful scenery in which to try this out. The road through the *barranco* then climbs upwards to the village of **San Bartolomé de Tirajana**.

Santa Lucía

The other route from the south begins heading this way from a number of points on the coastal motorway, all joining the C815 and leading up to the

attractive village of **Santa Lucía**, the centre of a busy fruit-farming area. Look out for the village church, with its unusual white dome. The area is also noted for the production of *mejunje*, a liqueur made of rum, honey and lemons. An attraction for tourists is the **Hao** Restaurant, which serves a variety of local Canarian dishes. The restaurateur also has a small private museum, the **Museo del Castillo de Fortaleza**, in a remarkable building resembling a small medieval castle. Its contents are a rag-bag of Guanche artefacts, which include pottery, implements, a couple of surprisingly well-preserved mummies and things such as stuffed birds and animals, pressed flowers and geological specimens. The museum is open from Monday to Saturday (08:00–20:00) and on Sunday (08:00–17:00).

Fortaleza Grande *

Santa Lucía's other attraction is **Fortaleza Grande**, a massive crenellated rock formation that looks like a castle, and which lies just to the south of the town and to the west of the C815. It was at this spot where, in 1483, the last defiant Guanches were persuaded by their former leader Tenesor Semidan to give themselves up and

Above: *Fertile terraces line the valley between Santa Lucia and San Bartolomé.*
Opposite: *The village of Fataga – situated on a bluff over a deep valley.*

TO TIP OR NOT TO TIP?

A tip (*una propina*) is always appreciated in the Canary Islands, but do not feel obliged to leave one unless the service is good. Check the bill to see if the service charge is included. If not, it is common to add between 5 and 10 per cent. In cafés and bars, some loose change is usually sufficient. Porters in hotels and airports generally expect a small tip. On excursions, coach drivers and guides are normally rewarded if they have provided good service.

Right: *The attractive façade of the parish church of San Bartolomé de Tirajana.*

Opposite Top: *Roque Nublo is the core of an ancient volcano. It can be seen from many parts of the island.*

Opposite Bottom: *This mobile snack bar is strategically parked at a popular roadside stop in the highlands.*

take up the Christian faith. Many refused and jumped off the rocks to their deaths below. The event is commemorated each year on 29 April. The road from Santa Lucía continues through to San Bartolomé.

FEATURES OF THE CENTRAL HIGHLANDS

The following sites and places can all be visited on a day trip using a hired car.

San Bartolomé de Tirajana

This attractive little town is actually the administrative centre for much of the southern part of the island, including the large coastal resorts such as Playa del Inglés. It is situated on the rim of an old volcanic crater, although this is not apparent when driving through this market town. Try to find time to look into the **Parish Church of Santiago**, with its three naves and attractive façade. A startling feature of the interior is the pair of statues of St James (Santiago) slaying a heathen. As with many towns in the highlands, **San Bartolomé** is famous for the production of a liqueur – in this case *Guindilla*, which is made from cherries, sugar and rum.

A few kilometres from San Bartolomé is the hamlet of **Ayacata**. Take the right turn here and just a short distance away there is a lay-by on the left-hand side of the road, usually with a mobile café in attendance.

Roque Nublo *

From here, a wide path, one of the *caminos reales* which formed a network of footpaths and donkey tracks, leads to the **Roque Nublo**. This slender spine of hard volcanic rock rises to 1813m (5948ft) and it is the second highest peak on the island. Roque Nublo, which is composed of basalt, is believed to have been the core of a volcano formed about 3.5 million years ago. Since then the forces of erosion, such as ice, rain and wind, have eroded away the softer surrounding material, leaving the core of the volcano as we see it today. The path leads right around the base of the rock and here there are other smaller spines, including one by

THE DURABLE CANARIAN PINE

The most common tree in this central region of Gran Canaria is the **Canarian pine** (*Pinus canariensis*). It is also the most useful tree, as it traps moisture from the wet trade winds: the water condenses on the pine needles and then falls to the ground, providing water for irrigation at lower levels. It also provides useful timber – the red heart of the trunk is used for building the ornate balconies that are typical of Canarian architecture. In addition, the Canarian pine is highly resistant to both forest fires and drought. The widespread felling of the pines is thought to have contributed to the drop in rainfall on the island, so it is encouraging to learn that in areas such as the **Tamadaba Natural Park** there is a comprehensive re-afforestation programme being implemented.

---

the name of **El Fraile** (the monk), as it looks like a monk at prayer. It is no surprise to learn that these rocks were sacred to the Guanches.

Pico de las Nieves *

The road continues from Roque Nublo and meets an intersection. Turn right here, travel through the pines and follow the signs to the **Pico de las Nieves** (the Peak of the Snows), which at 1949m (6395ft) is the highest point on the island. The site is a little disappointing, as a clutter of military communication aerials surround it, but the views are certainly breathtaking. On most days you are able to see the neighbouring island of Tenerife, with Mount Teide (the highest peak in Spain) rising above the clouds. There are also superb views over Las Palmas and the north of the island. The *pico* is named on many maps as the Pozo de las Nieves. A *pozo* is a well, and in the colder climates of the past, the water in the well near the summit was kept icy for much of the year. In summer, the ice was taken down to Las Palmas, where it served a number of functions. It is claimed to have been used in operations at the local hospital.

Opposite: *The Cruz de Tejeda. This stone cross once marked the centre of the* caminos *reales, or king's roads.*
Right: *Almond blossom makes an attractive sight in early spring.*

Cruz de Tejeda ★

The road back north is on the west of the summit. After 8km (5 miles) the hamlet of **Cruz de Tejeda** is reached at a busy crossroad. It is named after a cross of grey-green stone depicting the crucified Christ, which is supposed to mark the geographical centre of the island. This probably isn't true, but it certainly was the heart of the *caminos reales* (king's roads) that once formed a network around Gran Canaria (*see* page 118). Cruz de Tejeda comes as something of a shock after experiencing the serenity of the rest of the highlands. It is a popular coach stop and its somewhat tatty square is lined with rather pushy proprietors selling craft items, while souvenirs and donkey rides are also on offer here. Just across the square is a typical Canarian-style *parador* (a state-run hotel), which was built in the 1930s and designed by Néstor de la Torre. The hotel is currently closed, but it is possible to eat in the *parador's* restaurant and enjoy the beautiful views from its terrace. There is also a shop situated in the *parador* that sells a wide selection of authentic Canarian handicrafts.

WATER RESOURCES

Water is a scarce commodity on Gran Canaria and supplies come from the rainfall in the Central Highlands of the island. Much of the precipitation seeps into the ground and has to be recovered by digging wells. The water is then stored in tanks in order to satisfy the demand for agricultural irrigation. In recent years, the growth in tourism has increased the demand for water and since the main resorts are in the most arid parts of the island, drastic measures need to be taken. Firstly, a string of **reservoirs** have been constructed on the south side of the mountains, which – ironically – leads to water shortages in the mountain villages. Secondly, **desalinisation plants** have been built on the east coast.

CAMINOS REALES

Hiking paths in the mountains are not always common in Spanish-speaking countries, but in Gran Canaria there are a network of very old paths known as the *caminos reales* (king's roads). They are footpaths once maintained by royalty and were the usual routes before modern road transport came into being. They were frequently used for trading links and, by law, they had to be wide enough for two donkeys to pass. Not surprisingly, many have now become overgrown, but keen walking and environmental groups on the island are beginning to restore them and provide sign posts.

Artenara **

From Cruz de Tejeda it is worth taking the winding road to the village of **Artenara**, which – at 1270m (4166ft) – claims to be the highest settlement on Gran Canaria. The village seems fairly plain until you realise that behind the façades, the houses and shops extend into the hillside. The buildings even include a cave church known as the **Sanctuario de La Virgen de la Cuevita** and on 29 August the Virgen is celebrated with a night procession lit by torches. Head for Artenara's most distinct feature, the **Statue of Christ** on a hill at the edge of the town, which is reminiscent of the similar figure in Rio de Janiero. At the side of the hill a tunnel leads through the mountain to **La Silla** (The Chair), a cave restaurant located on a terrace with an overhanging rock roof. The view is magnificent, capturing both Roque Nublo and Roque Bentaiga. Take a look even if you do not intend to eat.

Tamadaba Natural Park *

Visitors who have plenty of time to spare should drive on past Artenara to the natural park, **Pinar de Tamadaba**, which is the largest area of forest in the Central Highlands. Many of the more mature trees are festooned with lichens and epiphytes that thrive in the damp conditions and frequent cloud cover. It is also evident that there has been an extensive Canary pine replanting programme. There are numerous picnic spots in the park and an idyllically situated camp site, but hardly any other facilities.

On your return, look out for the track to the right, which runs down past a string of reservoirs to **San Nicolás de Tolentino**. Although this scenic route is popular with jeep safaris, it should not be attempted without a four-wheel-drive vehicle. An alternative route back to the south coast along the C811 arrives at the village of **Tejeda**, which is set on a terrace overlooking a caldera. Tejeda is an agricultural settlement of only around 2000 inhabitants, as in recent years younger people have moved to the coast to work. The C811 skirts around the higher side of the village, but it is well worth making a diversion into the centre of Tejeda. The main street is like a tree-lined promenade, with wonderful views of both Roque Nublo and Roque Bentaiga. There is also an attractive square, numerous cobbled alleyways and an imposing white and grey church with two bell towers. The most common fruit grown here is the almond, and in the spring the village celebrates the *Almendra en flor* (the Festival of the Almond Blossom).

Opposite: *A huge statued Christ dominates the hill village of Artenara.*
Below: *Roque Bentaiga – a spine of basalt, once the core of an active volcano.*

Roque Bentaiga *

The journey back from Tejeda to San Bartolomé presents lovely views of **Roque Bentaiga**, another large volcanic spine, rising to the height of 1412m (4633ft). The surrounding area is an archaeological park and the region is rich in Guanche remains. A good example is the **Cueva del Rey** (the King's Cave) – a complex of both man-made and natural caves. There is an interpretation centre here, where visitors can learn about the geology, wildlife and natural history of the region.

The Central Highlands at a Glance

The central highland area of Gran Canaria is an all-year-round destination, although you should preferably try to visit the region on a cloud-free day. The central highlands can become cloudy when the prevailing trade winds are forced to rise up against the mountains. The cloud cover can be persistent and it may last for many days, particularly in the winter months. The highlands have more extreme temperatures than those areas along the coast, so be prepared for some high temperatures in summer and some very cold days in winter.

GETTING THERE

Public transport is limited in this region. There is only one Salcai **bus** per week from Playa del Inglés to the highlands, but a better service is provided from Las Palmas, where five Utinsa buses travel from the capital to Tejeda, via Santa Brígida and San Mateo, each day. **Coach** excursions to the highlands can be arranged with operators in the southern resorts.

GETTING AROUND

Coach excursions do include the main sites in their routes, but the most feasible option would be to **hire** a **car**, as it allows one the maximum freedom to explore the area. Hotel receptions are able to provide the names of reliable rental agencies. Remember that the roads are narrow and winding and often badly sign-posted. A very good road map is an essential require-ment for this region.

WHERE TO STAY

Accommodation in the high-lands is rather scarce, due to the proximity of the coast and Las Palmas. Visitors wishing to stay in the highlands for any length of time and who are interested in authentic and unusual properties could con-tact **RETUER**, an organization sponsoring **rural tourism**. They provide various kinds of accommodation in country farmhouses, cottages and even in cave houses. RETUER can be found at Calle Lourdes 2, Vega de San Mateo, 35320, Gran Canaria, tel: 928 661668, fax: 928 661560.

MID-RANGE
Molino de Fataga, Carretera Fataga at San Bartolomé Km I, tel: 928 172089. This delight-ful small hotel is housed in a converted *gofio* mill.

BUDGET
There are two excellent camp sites in the area:
Camping Temisas, Lomo de las Cruz, tel: 928 798149. This is a small camp site situated in a woodland setting on the road from Agüimes to San Bartolomé.

Camping Tamadaba, Pinar de Tamadaba. A superb site in the beautiful Pinar de Tamadaba Natural Park. Camping here is free of charge, but the only facility is running water.
Hostel Santana, Plaza Mayor San Bartolomé de Tirajana, tel: 928 127132. This is a simple *pension* situated close to the church.
Hotel El Refugio, Cruz de Tejeda s/n (located opposite the *parador* restaurant), tel: 928 666513, fax: 928 666520. This is a small and reasonably priced hotel, with traditional Canarian-style rooms. The *parador* at Cruz de Tejeda, closed at the time of writing, may have reopened by the time this book is published.

WHERE TO EAT

There is a wide choice of good restaurants in the country towns and villages of the highlands.

LUXURY
Hosteria Cruz de Tejeda, tel: 928 666050. A rather expensive *parador* restaurant serving local specialities such as roast kid. It is only open at midday.

MID-RANGE
La Esquina, Plaza de San Matias, Artenara. This is a good meat restaurant, which affords stunning views from its terrace.

The Central Highlands at a Glance

El Refugio, Cruz de Tejeda, tel: 928 666513. Hotel restaurant more reasonably priced than the *parador* across the road.

Restaurante Cueva de la Tea, Calle Dr.Hernández Guerra, Tejeda. Good meat restaurant near the southern exit to the village.

La Silla, Camino de la Silla 7, Artenara, tel: 928 658208. Surely the most spectacular setting for any restaurant in the Canaries.

Cho Zacarías, Avda Tinamar, San Mateo, tel: 928 660627. A lovely farmhouse setting situated just next to the Museum of Rural Life.

Budget

Restaurante Hao, Calle Tomas Arroyo Cardosa, Santa Lucía de Tirajana, tel: 928 798007. Be prepared to sit and eat at trestle tables and on hard benches. Open for lunch only.

Tours and Excursions

There are few, if any travel agencies in the highlands and most excursions in the area are arranged either in Las Palmas or in the southern coastal resorts. Coach tours tend to stop at Cruz de Tejeda, Pico de las Nieves and Artenara. The area is also popular for jeep safaris, and tours can be arranged from the southern resorts. For walking in the Central Highlands you will find that

the mountains provide the best hiking on the island, particularly along the *caminos reales*, used as trading routes in former times. A guidebook describing these parts can be bought in good bookshops on the island. For guided walks, contact **Grupo Montanero Mogan**, tel: 928 561204, which is an organization run by local enthusiasts and foreign residents.

Shopping

The villages of the central highlands of Gran Canaria are the strongholds of the island's craft industries, and there are good opportunities to buy products at reasonable prices from their source.

Liqueurs: a traditional liqueur of the central highlands is *Guindilla*, made with sour cherries. It can be bought at **Bar Martin**, **Calle Reyes Católicos** and **San Bartolomé de Tirajana**.

Almond Desserts: almond trees grow on the valley terraces of the central highlands and a number of shops sell traditional almond cakes and sweets. Try out **Dulceria Nublo**, Calle Dr. Mermández Guerra, Tejeda.

Pottery: Ceramics made in the traditional Guanche way can be found in the central highlands, particularly in the village of Santa Lucía de Tirajana. Two places where pottery can be bought are **Juan Ramírez**, Calle

Leopolde Matos 37, Santa Lucía de Tirajana, tel: 928 641389, and **Rozendo Lopez**, Calle Fernando Quanarteme 45, Santa Lucía de Tirajana, tel: 928 751298. Other **craft goods** available for sale include wooden objects, knives, basketwork, embroidery and a variety of musical instruments. All of these can be bought at the **FEDAC handicraft shop** at the Parador Cruz de Tejede. Beware of craft goods sold by African traders. Most of these craft goods are of African origin and they are not made by artisans from the Canary Islands. Moreover, many of these goods are made of ivory, leather or fur from endangered species. Buying such goods assists in the extermination of rare animals. and if you import these items into Europe or North America you could be subject to very heavy fines.

Useful Contacts

Note that there are no **tourist information offices** in the highlands and it is necessary to rely on those in Las Palmas and Playa del Inglés. For **camel rides** in the Fataga area contact **Camel Safari Park La Baranda**, Fataga Valley, tel: 928 798680 or **Manolos Camel Safaris**, Barranco de Arteara, tel: 928 798686. For **Megamoke Combi Tours** of the interior tel: 928 768479.

Travel Tips

Tourist Information

The **Spanish Tourist Board** has offices in the USA, in Canada, in Australia and in a host of non-English-speaking countries. In the United Kingdom, the address is: Spanish National Tourist Office, 22/23 Manchester Square, London, W1M 5AP, tel: (020) 7486 8077, fax: (020) 7486 8034. 24-hour request line: 0900 1669920. Web site: www.tourspain.co.uk There are local tourist board offices (ask for the *Oficina de Turismo*) on Gran Canaria in the following towns: **Las Palmas**, **Playa del Inglés**, **Puerto de Mogán** and **Puerto Rico**.

Entry Requirements

Visitors from Britain, USA, Canada, New Zealand and Australia must have valid passports. If staying for longer than three months, a visa from the Spanish Embassy in your native country is required. Visa extensions while on Gran Canaria must be applied for at the **Gobierno Civil** in Las Palmas. Anyone arriving by ferry with their own car needs their driving licence and international insurance Green Card.

Customs

The Canary Islands, despite being part of Spain, are not considered a member of the EU. The European Union abolished Duty Free Allowances in 1999, but at the time of writing certain limits remain on goods taken in and out of Gran Canaria. The **Duty Free Allowance** is: ALCOHOL – one litre of spirits; two litres of fortified wine and two litres of table wine; TOBACCO – 200 cigarettes or 50 cigars; PERFUME – 60cc or 250cc of toilet water and GIFTS – up to the value of £145 sterling.

Health Requirements

No vaccinations are necessary. Visitors from EU countries should bring Form E111 with them. This will entitle a degree of free medical treatment, but there is no substitute for good medical insurance.

Getting There

By Air: Cheap **charter flights** run to Gran Canaria from many European countries. Scheduled flights are more expensive and for international travellers this will mean using a route via London or Madrid, using **Iberia** or **British Airways**. International fights arrive at Gando airport in the south east of Gran Canaria. **By ship:** The only ferry (for both car and foot passengers) from Europe to Gran Canaria comes from Cádiz on mainland Spain.

What to Pack

There is no need to pack heavy clothing. A light jumper and wind-proof jacket are useful in the evenings and for trips to the mountains. For beach holidays, light sandals are recommended, as the volcanic sand can become very hot underfoot. Stronger footwear is needed for hiking in the mountains. The sun can be harsh throughout the year, so sunglasses and a sun hat are recommended. Don't forget sun-protection cream. Light, cotton clothes will prove most comfortable. Shorts and swimming costumes are essential for most holidaymakers. Ladies will find that a sarong is a highly adaptable item of clothing. Smarter casual clothing is needed for the evenings, particularly in hotels and expensive restaurants. Beachwear is unacceptable when visiting churches and cathedrals. Gran Canaria is a highly photogenic, so bring a camera or camcorder. Spare films are available.

Money Matters

Currency: The Euro was introduced on 1 January 2002, replacing the Spanish peseta, which was completely phased out on 28 February of that year. The fixed conversion rate at that time was 166 pesetas to the Euro. The Euro is split into 100 cents and there are coins to the value of 1, 2, 5, 10, 20 and 50 cents. There are also 1 and 2 Euro coins. Notes are issued to the value of 5, 10, 50, 100, 200, and 500 Euros.

Currency Exchange: Travellers' cheques and foreign currency can be cashed at banks, change outlets, post offices and hotels. Remember to have your passport when cashing travellers' cheques.

Banks: Finding a bank is not a problem, although the service might be slow. They are open on weekdays from 09:00 to 14:00 and Saturdays from 09:00 to 13:00. They charge a small amount of commission when cashing travellers' cheques, but usually give a better rate of exchange than most other places.

Credit Cards: The major credit cards are accepted throughout Gran Canaria in most shops, hotels, restaurants and exchange offices. There are automatic cash dispensers in all the larger towns and resorts, instructing in a variety of languages.

Tipping

A service charge is added to hotel and restaurant bills, so tipping is a matter of choice. A small gratuity for good service will be appreciated. Taxi drivers, guides and porters will expect a tip (*una propina*) of between 5 and 10 per cent.

Accommodation

Most of the accommodation on Gran Canaria caters for package tours, which means that the individual traveller who just turns up usually finds that the hotel or apartment block is fully booked. It is best, therefore, to book accommodation before arriving on the island. There is a vast range of **hotels** from luxury five-star establishments to modest one-star boarding houses. **Aparthotels** have the usual facilities, but have some self-catering rooms. **Apartments** far outnumber hotels and they are usually cheaper and have similar facilities, such as pools, bars and restaurants. Most of the apartments are self-catering, but at the same time they encourage you to sample the food in local restaurants. There are three good **campsites** in Gran Canaria, all in attractive areas. Unofficial camping, particularly on beaches, is not

---

ROAD SIGNS

Traffic symbols in Gran Canaria are those used throughout the EU and they are internationally recognized. The road signs include:

Alto • Stop
Camino Cerrado • Road Closed
Cedo el Paso • Give Way
Circunvalación • By-pass
Curva Peligrosa • Dangerous Bend
Derecha • Right
Derecho • Straight On
Despacio • Slow
Dirrumbes en la Via • Beware of rock falls
Dirrecion Unica • One Way
Izquierdo • Left
No Adelantar • No Overtaking
No Estacionar/Parquero • No Parking
No Hay Paso • No Entrance
Peligro • Danger
Reduzca Velocidad • Reduce Speed
Salida • Exit
Semáforo • Traffic Lights
Trabajos en la Via • Roadworks

---

encouraged. **Casas Rurales** are converted farmhouses or village properties that make an attractive option for those who wish to get away from the bustle and noise of the large resorts. Advanced booking is essential. Gran Canaria is an all-year-round tourist destination, with its peak season between December and March when the climate is a better option to those from northern Europe. At this time of the year accommodation will be at its most expensive and it is most likely to be fully booked.

USEFUL PHRASES

Yes • *Si*
No • *No*
Please • *Por favor*
Thank you • *Gracias*
Hello • *Hola*
Goodbye • *Adios*
See you later • *Hasta Luego*
My name is... • *Me Llamo...*
Do you speak English? •
Habla (usted) Inglés?
You're welcome • *De nada*
I don't speak Spanish • *No hablo Español*
How much is...? • *Cuánto cuesta...?*
Do you have...? • *Tiene...?*
Please speak more slowly • *Hablé más despacio, por favor*
Where is...? • *Donde está...?*
What time does it arrive/leave? • *A qué hora sale/llega?*
It's too expensive • *Es demasiado caro*
Do you have anything cheaper? • *No tiene algo más barato?*
Is there...? • *Hay...?*
Please fill the tank • *Llénelo del todo, por favor*
Is there a hotel near here? • *Hay un hotel por aqui?*

Summer is also busy and it is during this period that the mainland Spaniards travel to Gran Canaria. Low season prices for accommodation tend to be in May and November.

Transport

Air: There are inter-island flights from Gran Canaria to all the other Canary Islands.

Ferries: All the islands in the group are supplied with regular ferry services, mostly run by Compania Trasmediterranea or Lineas Fred Olsen.

Buses: Known as *guaguas*, buses provide a comprehensive service around the island. The green-coloured Salcai buses cover the south, including the airport, while the orange and blue Utinsa buses provide services for the north and centre of the island.

Car Hire: Car hire rates on Gran Canaria are just about the cheapest in Europe and with a good, well signposted road system, the rental of a car can add much to the enjoyment of a holiday. Most of the international rental firms have offices at the airport. An **International Driving Permit** is required in theory, but most firms accept a valid national driving licence.

Driving Hints: In Gran Canaria you drive on the right, overtake on the left and give way to traffic from the right at roundabouts. Carry your driving licence and passport (or a photocopy) when driving, as the police can demand to see them. Seat belts should be worn at all times, including those in the rear seats. It is prohibited to use a mobile phone when driving and it is also forbidden to throw objects out of the window. The blood alcohol limit is 0.08 per cent and any driver involved in an accident can expect to undergo a Breathalyzer test. Police are able to impose on-the-spot fines to non-resident drivers, but the good news is that there is a 20 per cent discount if the fine is paid immediately.

Speed limits are 120kph (75mph) on motorways, 100kph (62mph) on dual carriageways and 90kph (56mph) on other roads. There is a speed limit of 60kph (37mph) in built-up areas. A motorway (*autopista*) runs from Aguineguín in the south to Las Palmas and then along the north coast where it will eventually connect with Agaete. Despite some tricky winding roads in the west, it is perfectly possible to drive right around the island in a day, although this would exclude the interior. Progress on some of the inland roads, however, is slow. **Parking** is scarce, particularly in Las Palmas, and the motorist is advised to use the underground car parks available. Pay and display areas are marked with blue kerb lines. Cars parked illegally are quickly towed away and it can be expensive, time-consuming and frustrating to recover the vehicle. Breakdowns are usually caused by overheating and motorists should take spare water and oil on longer journeys. In the event of an accident involving a hired car, report the incident to the rental agency immediately. Petrol stations are widespread in Gran Canaria and most accept credit cards. Fuel is cheaper than in mainland Spain and the rest of Europe. It is advisable to have a good map of Gran Canaria if driving around the island. Tourist offices provide adequate maps, but for more detailed maps, try the bookshops. They offer road maps, which include town street plans. The *Globetrotter Travel Map* of Gran Canaria is highly recommended.

Taxis: Gran Canaria's taxis are good value by European standards. They are generally in the form of a white Mercedes and show a plate with the letters SP (*Servicio Publico* – Public Service). They are metered for short journeys, but for longer trips you should negotiate the fare. A green light on the roof shows if the taxi is free for hire.

Business Hours

On weekdays, offices, post offices and most shops are open between 09:00 and 13:00, and after the siesta period between 16:00 and 19:00. On Saturday they are open between 09:00 and 13:00. Food stores and super-markets (*supermercados*) may open for longer periods, while some shops in the tourist resorts may open on Sundays.

Time Difference

Gran Canaria, and the rest of the Canary Islands, maintain Greenwich Mean Time in the winter months, so there is a one-hour time difference with mainland Europe. Clocks are set back one hour in summer.

Communications

Telephones: The old three-figure regional digits have now been incorporated into the telephone numbers, so that you have to dial all nine numbers even if phoning within the same town. If mak-ing an international call, dial

00 first and then the country code, followed by the area code (omitting the first 0) and then the number. If dialling Gran Canaria from abroad, the country code is 34, the same as the rest of Spain. There are plenty of the dis-tinctive blue telephone booths, which take both phone cards and cash. The phone cards (*tarjetas telefóni-cas*) can be bought at post offices and tobacconists. If making expensive long-distance calls, it is best to use the large cabins or *locutorios*. You pay at the desk on leaving and credit cards are accepted.

Mobile Phones: Mobile phones operating on the usual GSM European MHz work in the Canary Islands.

Post: Post boxes (*buzons*) are yellow in colour. Stamps (*sell-os*) are sold at post offices (*oficinas de correos*) and also at newsagents and shops sell-ing postcards. Post offices open during normal office hours. The postal service is rather slow and inefficient. Allow a week for a card to reach Europe, 10 days for North America and two

weeks for Australia, New Zealand and South Africa.

Fax: Most hotels provide a fax service free of charge.

Internet: Cyber cafés have begun to appear, but are mainly confined to Las Palmas and the resorts in the south.

Electricity

The electrical current in Gran Canaria is 220 volts, although some hotels have 110 volts for electric razor sockets. Plugs have two round pins in line with most of Europe. Bring adapters for your appliances and buy them before leaving home, as it is unlikely you will find them in Gran Canaria.

Weights and Measures

The metric system is used both in Gran Canaria and in the rest of the Canary Islands.

Health Services

Citizens of EU countries are entitled to free medical treat-ment on production of Form E111, which should be obtained before travelling. Form E111 does not, however, cover medical prescriptions or dental treatment. Gran Canaria

CONVERSION CHART		
FROM	**TO**	**MULTIPLY BY**
Millimetres	Inches	0.0 394
Metres	Yards	1.0936
Metres	Feet	3.281
Kilometres	Miles	0.6214
Square kilometres	Square miles	0.386
Hectares	Acres	2.471
Litres	Pints	1.760
Kilograms	Pounds	2.205
Tonnes	Tons	0.984
To convert Celsius to Fahrenheit: x 9 ÷ 5 + 32		

PUBLIC HOLIDAYS

The following public holidays are **fixed dates**:
1 January • New Year's Day (*Año Nuevo*)
6 January • Epiphany (*Epifanía*) or Three Kings Day (*Día de los Reyes Magos*), when children are given presents.
19 March • Saint Joseph's Day (*Día de San José*)
1 May • Labour Day (*Día del Trabajo*)
30 May • Canary Islands Day (*Día de las Islas Canarias*)
25 July • Feast of Saint James the Apostle (*Día de Santiago Apóstol*)
15 August • Assumption Day (*Asunción*)
12 October • Day of the Spanish Speaking World (*Día de la Hispanidad*)
1 November • All Saints' Day (*Todos Santos*)
6 December • Constitution Day (*Día de la Constitución*)
8 December • Feast of the Immaculate Conception (*La Immaculada Concepción*)
25 December • Christmas (*Navidad*)
In addition there are a number of **movable feast days**. These are Maunday Thursday, Good Friday, Easter Day, Whitsun, Ascension Day and Corpus Christi. Note that Boxing Day, Easter Monday and Whit Monday are not public holidays in Gran Canaria. In addition, there are **regional fiestas** that are also local holidays. Consult local tourist offices for full details.

has some good **hospitals** and a host of **private clinics** with English-speaking staff. Hotel receptions can usually provide the name of an English-speak-

ing doctor (*medico*). Minor medical problems can usually be solved by visiting a **chemist** (*farmacia*). Pharmacists in Spain give advice and are allowed to dispense a wide variety of prescription drugs. *Farmacias* are open during normal shop hours and are distinguished by an illuminated green cross. In a large town at least one pharmacy will be open after normal hours with a duty rota displayed in the window. The **Red Cross** (*Cruz Roja*) often provides small medical centres on beaches in the main resorts. Services for the **disabled traveller** are generally poor in Gran Canaria, particularly in public transport and toilets.

Health Precautions

Most visitors to Gran Canaria experience few health problems. Hygiene requirements are strict and food poisoning is rare. The biggest danger is overexposure to the sun, resulting in **sunburn** and **dehydration**. Wear a sun hat and good quality sunglasses and avoid exposure during the hottest parts of the day. To

avoid dehydration drink plenty of liquids. The main symptoms of heatstroke are nausea, headaches and increased heartbeats. Treat initially with rehydrating solutions containing sugar, salt and water.

Personal Safety

Crime statistics are low in Gran Canaria, with the exception of parts of Las Palmas. Local authorities realise that crime figures can affect tourist trade, so the police keep a high profile in order to keep the island safe. Nevertheless, petty crime does exist, mainly in the form of bag snatching and theft from cars.

Emergencies

To call the **police**, dial **091** and for **medical** emergencies requiring an ambulance, **062**.

Etiquette

Topless sunbathing is common at beaches and pools, but full nudity is frowned upon and only tolerated at certain locations. Beachwear is not acceptable when visiting churches and cathedrals.

GOOD READING

Concepción, José Luis (1984) *The Guanches – survivors and their descendents*. A sympathetic account of the early inhabitants of the Canary Islands. Ediciones Graficolor, La Laguna, Tenerife.
Fernández-Armesto, Felipe (1982) *The Canary Islands After the Conquest*. A specialized history of the islands in the 16th century. Clarendon, Oxford.
Sánchez-Pinto, Lázaro and de Saá, Lucas (1993) *Flora of the Canary Islands*. A handbook and map in folder form. Ediciones Turquesa, Santa Cruz, Tenerife.
Walker, Ann and Larry *Pleasures of the Canary Islands: Wine, Food, Beauty, Mystery*. Particularly good on cooking. Hardback.
Clarke, Tony and Collins, David (1996) *A Birdwatcher's Guide to the Canary Islands*. Prion, UK.

INDEX

Note: Numbers in **bold**
indicate photographs

accommodation 47, 51,
   52, 68, 73–74, 81, 84,
   85, 95, 96–97, 107,
   117, 120, 123–124
Agaete 99, **104**–105
agriculture 18–**20**, 22, **23**,
   24, 39, 55, **56**, 71, 80,
   83, 109, 117
Agüimes 71, 72, **78**–80
Anden Verde 99
architecture 23, 31, 34–35,
   40, 56, 63, 65, 78
   Gothic 41
   Mudéjar **34–35**, 46, 76,
   106
   Plateresque 35, 41
Arguineguín 92
art galleries 43
   Centro Atlántico de Arte
   Moderno 33, 44
Artenara **108**, 109,
   110, 118
Arucas 55

Bahía Feliz 84
Bañaderos 56
barrancos (ravine) 5, 8, 55,
   56, 61, 62, 72, 79, 93,
   94, 99, 102, 109, 112
   Barranco de Fataga 112
   Barranco de Guayadeque
   5, 71, 72, 78, **79**
   Barranco de Mogán 100
   Barranco de Moya 62
   Guiniguada Barranco 72
   Valle del Barranco de
   Aldea **102**
beaches
   Playa de Veneguera
   99, 101
   Playa de la Aldea 99, 103
   Playa de las Alcaravaneras
   49
   Playa de las Canteras **8**,
   9, 37, 38, **50**
   Playa del Águila 84
   Playa del Cardón 9
   Playa del Cura 94
   Playa del Inglés 5, 39, 83,
   84, 85–86, 109
botes (service boats) 45
British 16, 20, **29**, 39, 74
buses **47**

cabildos (island councils) 19
Caldera de Bandama 71,
   74–75
Caminos Reales 118
Canarios (see Guanches)
capital (see Las Palmas)
Carthaginians 13
Casa del Conde de la Vega
   76
Casa Regental 41
casinos 47
Castillo de la Luz
caves **33**, 59, **79**
   Cenobio de Valerón 55,
   58–**59**
   Cueva del Rey 119
   Cueva Pintada 14, 42,
   55, **58**, 59–60
   Cuevas de los Frailes 73
   Embalse de la Cueva de
   las Niñas 101
   La Silla 118
   Sanctuario de La Virgen
   de la Cuevita 118
César Manrique 63, 102
charca (lagoon) 9
churches 35, 55, **114**, 119
   Arucas 55
   Basílica de la Virgen del
   Pino 64
   Catedral de Santa Ana **4**,
   5, 37, **40**–41
   Chapel of San Antonio
   Abad 44
   Church of Our Lady of
   Candelaria 77
   Church of Santa María
   56
   Church of Santiago de los
   Caballerosare 57
   Ecumenical Church of San
   Salvador 85
   Ermita de San Telmo 45
   Iglesia de la Concepción
   104
   Iglesia el Pilar 62
   Iglesia San Francisco 46
   Iglesia San Juan Bautista,
   Arucas 65, **66**
   Iglesia San Juan Bautista,
   Telde 71, **76**
   Parish Church of Santiago
   114
   San Antonio Abad 43
   Sanctuario de La Virgen
   de la Cuevita 118
climate 9–10, 41, 56, 73,
   84, 101, 110
coach excursions 6

Columbus, Christopher 18,
   43, 44
communications 125
crafts **31**–**32**, 39, 57,
   61, 117
Cro-Magnon man 13
Cruz de Tejeda 111, **117**
Cuatro Puertas 72
cueva (see caves)
currency 6, 13, 123

de Béthencourt, Jean 15
de la Torre, Néstor Martín
   Férnandez 44, 46
Dedo de Dios 99, 106
drink 18, 29–**30**, 31,
   63, 115
driving 37, 123, 124
dunes 5, 9

economy **14**, 18–20, 22–23
El Agüero 60
El Fraile 116
El Hierro 6
El Risco 104
embalse (see reservoirs)
emergencies 126
emigration 21, 37
Ermita de Nuestra Señora
   de las Nieves 106
Estación de Guaguas 45
European Union 13

Fataga 112
fauna 6, 11–**12**, 28, 61,
   89, 90–**91**, 92
   dogs **16**, 17
faycan (Guanche priest)
   14, 15
Fernando León y Castillo
   19, 39
festivals 13, 24–25, 119,
   126
   Bajada de la Rama 105
   Corpus Christi 42, 43
fishing 9, 26, 61, 94, 105
flag **22**
flora 6, **10**–**11**, **19**, 71, 74,
   90–91, 102, 104–105,
   116, 119
   cactus 73
   Canary palm 77
   Canary pine 73
   dragon tree 11, 15, 74
food 14, 26, **27**–**28**, 29,
   46, 57, 91, 100,
   106, **115**
   gofio 14, 27
   papas arrugadas 27

Fortaleza Grande 109,
   110, 113
Franco 20, 39
Fuerteventura 6, 7,
   13,15,19, 39

Gáldar 6, 14, 55, 57, 59
gardens 84, 100
   Cuidad Jardín 48
   Huerto de las Flores 104
   Jardín Botánico Canario
   70, 71, 72–**73**, 74
government 21–22
guanatemes (Guanche king)
   14, 15
Guanches 6, 13, 14, **15**,
   16, 17, 32, 33, 34, 38,
   42, 43, 55, 57, 58, 59,
   61, 71, 73, 75, 79, 110,
   113, 116, 119
Guía 56

health 122, 125–126
history 13–21
Hoya de Pineda 61

Idolo de Tara **75**, 77
information 53, 69, 81,
   107, 121, 122
Ingenio 71, 72, 77–78

La Calzada 73
La Gomera 6, 13, 15
La Isleta 38
La Palma 6, 7, 16
land 6–12
language 6, 17
Lanzarote 6, 7, 13, 15, 19,
   39
Las Dunas de Maspalomas
   5
Las Palmas 6, 8, 9, 13, 18,
   23, **36**, **39**, **43**, **44**,
   37–51, 61, 63, 71, 74
   Alcaravaneras 48
   Arenales 47
   La Isleta 51
   Lugo 47
   Santa Catalina 49
   Triana 39, 44–47
   Vegueta 39–44
León y Castillo, Juan 77, 78
literature 33, 126
   Galdós, Benito Pérez 48
   Morales, Tomás 61, 62
Los Azulejos 101
Los Tilos 62
Luján Pérez, José 33, 40,
   41, 55, 56, 57, 65, 76

Macronesia 6
markets 44, 111
Maspalomas 5, 9, 82, 83,
    86–88, 92, 109
Miguel Martín Fernández de
    la Torre 40, 46
mirador (see viewpoints)
Mogán 83, 99, 100
Montaña de las Cuatro
    Puertas 77
Moors 16
mountains 6, 7–8, 109,
    114, 119
  Mount Teide 104
  Pico de Bandama 6, 74
  Pico de Gáldar 57
  Pico de las Nieves 5, 116
Moya 62
museo (see museums)
museums 6, 33, 56
  Casa de Colón 33, 37,
    43, 44
  Casa Museo Cho' Zacarias
    111
  Casa Museo Patrones de
    la Virgen del Pino 65
  Casa Museo Pérez Galdós
    46
  Casa Museo Tomás
    Morales 62
  Mundo Arborigen 112
  Museo Canario 5, 15, 33,
    37, 42, 60, 75, 79
  Museo de Piedras y
    Artesanía 78
  Museo del Castillo de
    Fortaleza 113
  Museo Diocesano de Arte
    Sacro 41
  Museo León y Castillo 76
  Museo Néstor 48
music 33, 34, 56

NASA Space Tracking
    Station 92
Necropolis 60

paintings 33, 40, 43, 46
Palacio Episcopal
parks
  Parque de San Telmo 45
  Parque de Santa Catalina
    48, 49
  Parque Doramas 47
parque (see parks)

Paseo Costa Canario 85
Pasito Blanco 92
Patalavaca 92
people 23–35
Phoenicians 13
Pinar de Tamadaba Natural
    Park 104
Playa de Sardina **61**
Playa del Inglés
    (see beaches)
playas (see beaches)
policemen 22
political parties 21
population 6, 23, 37, 39
ports
  Puerto de la Luz 38,
    50–51
  Puerto de las Nieves **98**,
    99, 105–**106**
  Puerto de Mogán 83, **94**,
    95, 100, 101
  Puerto Nuevo 94
  Puerto Rico 9, **93**–94
  Puerto San Nicolás 103
  Puerto Sardina 55
Pozo Izquierdo 84
Pueblo Canario 40
puertos (see ports)

Real de las Palmas 38
Rejón, Juán 38
religion 6, 24, **25**
  Christianity 16, 17, 24
  Islam 24
  Judaism 24
reservoirs 8, 117, 118
  Embalse Caidero de la
    Niña 103
  Embalse de Parralillo 103
  Embalse de Siberio 103
  Embalse del Mulato 101
resorts 9
  Costa Canaria 83
  Playa del Inglés (see
    beaches)
  San Agustín 84
restaurants **29**, 49, 52–53,
    61, 63, 68–69, 73, 74,
    81, 85, 93, 97, 105,
    107, 113, 118, 120–121
rivers 7–8
Roque Bentaiga 8, 15, 109,
    118, **119**
Roque Nublo 7, 8, 15, 109,
    115–116, 118

safety 39
San Agustín 83
San Bartolomé de Tirajana
    112, **113**, **114**–115
San Fernando 86
San Francisco 75, 76
San Juan 75
San Mateo 111
San Nicolás de Tolentino
    99, 100, 102, 118
Santa Brígida 45, 71,
    74, 110
Santa Lucía 112–**113**
Santa María de Guía 55
sculpture 33, 40, 55, 56,
    63, 76, 100
shopping 53, 69, 81,
    121, 125
  Centro Yumbo 85
  El Corte Inglés 49
Spanish Civil War 39, 45
Spanish Colonial Rule
    17–18
Spanish Conquest, The 6,
    10, 13, 15–17, 34, 75
sport 25–**26**, 83, 95
  deep-sea fishing 94
  football 26
  go-karting 89
  golf 74, 76
  hiking 5, 100
  sail boarding 9, 94
  sailing 5, 26
  scuba diving 9, 26
  snorkelling 26
  surfing 9
  swimming 93
  volleyball 26
  waterskiing 26, 94
  windsurfing 5, 26
squares
  Parque de Santa Catalina
    37
  Plaza de Colón 44, 46
  Plaza de España 49
  Plaza de Nuestra Señora
    del Pino 64
  Plaza de Santa Ana
    16, 41
  Plaza Teresa de Bolívar 65
Statue of Christ **118**
sugar-press monument **77**

Tafira Alta 71, 73
Tafira Baja 71, 72

Tafiras 110
Tamadaba Natural Park
    109, 118–119
Tasarte 102
Tasartico 102
Taurito 94
Tauro 94
Teatro Pérez Galdós
    40, 46
Tejeda 110, **111**, 119
Telde 6, 14, 71, 75, 76–77
Tenerife 6, 7, 13, 15, 16,
    17, 19, 71
Teror 5, 6, **54**, 55, 63,
    64–**65**
theme parks 5, 83, 88–92
  Aqua Sur 89
  Holiday World 89
  Mundo Aborigen 91–92
  Océano Parque Acuatico
    Maspalomas 89
  Palmitos Park 83, **90**–**91**
  Parque de Cocodrilos
    71, 78
  Reptilandia 55, 61, **62**
  Sioux City 83, 88–89
time 6, 125
Tocodomán 102
tourism 6, 21, 22, 39, 80
tours 53, 69, 81,
    107, 121
trade winds 5, 9, 10,
    71, 73
transport 6, 47, 51, 52, 68,
    81, 96, 107, 112, 120,
    122, 124
Tumuló de la Guancha
    (see Necropolis)

University of Gran Canaria
    72, 74

Vecindario 84
Vega de San Mateo
    110–111
Veneguera 101
viewpoints
  Mirador Balcón de Zamora
    63, 112
  Mirador del Balcón 99,
    103–104
Virgen del Pino 64, 65
volcanoes 6, 7, 8, 10,
    55, 57, 91, 104, 109,
    111, **119**